D0126029

MODERN TRACK AND FIELD FOR

GIRLS AND WOMEN

Donnis Hazel Thompson

Associate Professor
University of Hawaii

Allyn and Bacon, Inc.
Boston • London • Sydney • Toronto

Library of Congress Catalog Card No.: 72–85178

Fifth printing . . . July, 1976

ISBN: 0-205-03255-9

Dedication

To my colleagues as they mature toward the full realization that programs and leadership must be provided now so that each person is allowed and encouraged to reach his or her fullest potential regardless of race or sex. Those things worth having are worth having now.

Contents

Foreword   **ix**

Preface   **xiii**

Introduction   **1**

Unique for Girls and Women; Participation
Outside of Class

PART I: TRACK EVENTS   **5**

Chapter 1   Starting   **7**

Description; Mechanical Principles Operative at Critical
Parts of Starting; Common Errors and Corrections;
Teaching Progression; Rules

Chapter 2   Sprinting   **17**

Description; Mechanical Principles Operative at Critical
Parts of Sprinting; Common Errors and Corrections;
Teaching Progression; Rules; Strategy

Chapter 3   Middle-Distance Running   **28**

Description; Mechanical Principles; Common Errors and
Corrections; Teaching Progression; Rules; Strategy

Chapter 4   Cross-Country Running   **32**

Description; Mechanical Principles Operative at Critical
Parts of Distance Running; Common Errors and
Corrections; Teaching Progression; Rules; Strategy

Chapter 5   Relay Racing   **39**

Description; Conventional Nonvisual Pass; Sprint Pass;
Visual Pass; Common Errors and Corrections; Teaching
Progression; Rules; Strategy

Chapter 6   Hurdling   **54**

Description; Mechanical Principles Operative at Critical
Parts of Hurdling; Common Errors and Corrections;
Teaching Progression; Rules; Strategy

PART II: FIELD EVENTS   65

Chapter 7   Long Jump   **67**

Description; Mechanical Principles Operative at Critical
Parts of the Long Jump; Common Errors and Corrections;
Teaching Progression; Rules; Strategy

Chapter 8   High Jump   **80**

Description; Mechanical Principles Operative at Critical
Parts of the High Jump; Common Errors and Corrections;
Teaching Progression; Rules

Chapter 9   Shot Put   **92**

Description; Mechanical Principles Operative at Critical
Parts of the Shot Put; Common Errors and Corrections;
Teaching Progression; Rules

Chapter 10   Discus   **101**

Description; Mechanical Principles Operative at Critical
Parts of the Discus Throw; Common Errors and
Corrections; Teaching Progression; Rules

Chapter 11   Javelin   **111**

Description; Mechanical Principles Operative at Critical
Parts of the Javelin Throw; Common Errors and
Corrections; Teaching Progression; Rules

PART III: TEACHING AND COACHING   121

Chapter 12   Teaching Methods and Techniques   **123**

Description; Planning Units and Lessons; References;
Sample Teaching Unit (Secondary School Level), 141;

Sample Lesson Plan: Relay (Nonvisual Pass) (Secondary School Level), 162

Chapter 13 Coaching Methods and Techniques **169**

General Training Principles; Developmental Factors in Training; Strategy for Competition

PART IV: ORGANIZATIONAL AND ADMINISTRATIVE FACTORS **181**

Chapter 14 Attire, Facilities, Equipment, Supplies **183**

Attire; Official Equipment and Supplies; Facilities; Equipment; Supplies

Chapter 15 Organizing a Track and Field Meet **188**

Meet Director; Officials; Head Groundsman; Ticket Manager; Program Editor; Public Relations; Responsibilities During the Meet; Postmeet Responsibilities

Chapter 16 Officiating Techniques **198**

Qualities of a Good Official; Officials for a Meet

Bibliography **214**

Appendices **217**

Appendix A: Equipment and Supply Companies   218
Appendix B: Films, Audiovisuals Aids   219
Appendix C: English Equivalents of Metric Distances   221
Appendix D: Point Scores for Track and Field
         Performances   222
Appendix E: Weight Training Exercises   224
Appendix F: Weight Training Schedule   229
Appendix G: Isometric Exercises   231
Appendix H: Calisthenic Exercises   233
Appendix I: Annual Training Schedules   242

Index **269**

Foreword

The Allyn and Bacon Sports Education Series

Today, sports are playing a major role in the life of practically every American: the educated and non-educated, the advantaged and dis-advantaged, the handicapped and non-handicapped. Our fast-growing involvement in sports is manifested principally in two different ways: through *participation* as players, coaches or officials and through *observation* as spectators at sports events—on the scene or through television, radio, and movies.

The increased interest in sports is the result of several trends. Many people have more leisure time because laborers, office personnel and people in the professions work fewer and fewer hours per week.

Another trend is the increased emphasis on physical fitness. Automation, labor saving devices, and the mechanization of many industries are responsible for reducing the amount of physical activity among people today. As a result, many people need to become active in order to be physically fit. It is interesting to note, however, that today's advocates of physical fitness recommend sports participation rather than formal exercise or calisthenics. Sports are more in keeping with the culture and philosophy of our country. The *President's Council on Physical Fitness and Sports* stresses the need for such activity to bring about physical fitness.

Interest in sports is also being promoted by the increase in television and radio broadcasts. Sports such as hockey, gymnastics, and soccer—currently not familiar to the general public—are, and will continue to be, presented and explained. Broadcasts of team sports, such as football, basketball, and baseball, as well as of the lifetime sports, including tennis and golf, will be expanded. There will be more programs on which sport skills will be analyzed and strategy will be discussed by knowledgeable commentators using techniques such as stop action and instant video replay.

An important result of this increased emphasis on sports in American life is the need for improved literature—literature not only to guide the participant and coach in our rapidly developing sports and recreation programs, but also to inform the spectator about the strategy, tactics, and techniques involved.

The *Allyn and Bacon Sports Education Series* has been created in response to this need. Each book is designed to provide an in-depth treatment of a selected sport for students majoring in physical education and for people in other fields who would like to coach. Young men and women who are beginning their coaching careers, as well as experienced coaches, will find great value in the books. It will be noted that reference is made to *both* men and women: even though some of the volumes will be used exclusively either by men or by women, most of the books are designed for use by both. The books also provide a source of information to spectators. They can become more knowledgeable about and appreciative of the basic and finer aspects of sports.

The authors have been carefully selected. They include experienced coaches of high school, college, and professional teams, outstanding sportsmen, and physical educators from teacher's colleges and universities. Some books represent the combined effort of two authors, each with a different background and each contributing particular strengths to the text. For other books, a single author has been selected, whose background offers a breadth of knowledge and experience in the sport being covered.

Among our co-authors are Bob Cousy, an outstanding college coach and former professional player, and Frank Power, a successful high school coach. They wrote the volume on basketball. The result of this collaboration is a combination of drills, techniques, and coaching tips that will be helpful to both high school and college students of the game.

Professor Mildred Barnes of the University of Iowa and Professor Kitty Kjeldsen of the University of Massachusetts, leading experts on women's physical education activities, developed books on field hockey and women's basketball and gymnastics.

Jack Barnaby, the successful tennis coach of Harvard University, authored the book on tennis. Mr. Barnaby has also taught boys and girls during the summer months for many years and thus combines a background of teaching and coaching.

This Sports Series will enable readers to experience the thrills of the sport from the point of view of participants and coaches, to learn some of the reasons for success and causes of failure, and to receive basic information about teaching and coaching techniques.

Each volume in the series reflects the philosophy of the authors, but a common theme runs through all: the desire to instill in the reader knowledge and appreciation of sports and physical activity which will carry over throughout his life as a participant or a spectator.

The general topics within each volume include a background of the sport, skill drills, practice sessions, rules of the game, and specific coaching techniques and strategy. Pictures, drawings, and diagrams are used throughout each book to clarify and illustrate the discussion.

Some books include related references and sources for audiovisual aids, such as films, film strips, and loop films.

The reader, whether beginner or experienced in sports, will gain much from each book in this in-depth *Allyn and Bacon Sports Education Series.*

Arthur G. Miller
Department of Physical Education
Boston University

Preface

This book was written for those who teach and coach track and field in all kinds of programs. It is a resource book for physical education students and majors who are interested in gaining skill as well as a greater understanding of sound track fundamentals to be used later in imparting their knowledge to others.

The book begins with a general overview and explanation of the uniqueness of this sport and participation possibilities within and beyond the physical education class.

In Part I the skills and events presented are starting, sprinting, middle-distance and distance running, high and low hurdles, and relay racing. Each chapter covers the complete development of each of these events and skills.

Part II has two main divisions: The first discusses jumping events—long jump and high jump; the second includes weight or throwing events, the shot put, the discus, and the javelin. These events are grouped into these two categories because of their many features: methods of teaching, application of scientific principles, terminology, training techniques, rules governing the event, and strategies related to the competitive situation.

Part III contains general methods and techniques of teaching and coaching which are applicable to all physical activities; however, in this section their utilization relating specifically to track and field is discussed. Chapter 12, "Teaching Methods and Techniques," includes material for both the beginning and more experienced teacher. This chapter also presents an in-depth method of gathering and planning learning experiences related to track and field, a resource unit, a teaching unit, and a sample lesson plan. Specific information in Chapter 13 provides a fuller understanding of the principles related to training and competition, as well as general strategy for competition. Since training is frequently understood merely as repeated physical exercises, the intent of this chapter is to attach a broader meaning and understanding to the term *training*. Chapter 13 has been developed for the coach.

Part IV, *Organizational and Administrative Factors,* is included for those involved in meet planning and/or officiating. It cites specific responsibiilties of personnel before, during, and after the meet. One discussion relates to the selection and care of wearing apparel, official and improvised equipment, supplies, and facilities.

The Bibliography will be helpful to the reader who seeks additional information related and applicable to track and field.

The appendices are extensive and supplemental to the text. They contain information about practice schedules for each event; companies where equipment and supplies may be purchased; films and other audiovisual aids with sources; descriptions and illustrations of weight training exercises, isometric exercises, and calisthenics; and point scores in the evaluation of track and field performance.

A special acknowledgment is extended to Chi Cheng, Wyllie B. White, Mamie Rollins, Doris Brown, and Pam Kilborn. It was through personal conversations with these superior athletes that the author was able to make this book functional for the sophisticated coach and participant.

Donnis Hazel Thompson
University of Hawaii

Introduction

UNIQUE FOR GIRLS AND WOMEN

Track and field may involve all levels of participation—from the woman who wishes to maintain physical fitness by running to the female athlete who wants to become an accomplished international performer. The old-fashioned and unfounded concepts of masculinity in sports and the frailness of the female are quickly disappearing. On television and in newspapers and magazines, the greatest female athletes may be seen in national and international competitions. Seen before, during, and after the heat of competition, today's accomplished women athletes are attractive, charming, shapely, fashion-conscious, and assets to the female image. If such accomplished athletes can remain feminine throughout the grueling physical and mental preparations that are necessary to earn championships, the average female seeking such experiences should not fear losing her femininity because of competitive participation.

The idea of the "fragile" woman has been developed through culture. Historically, the woman's role was always subordinate to the man's, regardless of the amount of activity her job required. Physical education programs followed this trend by emphasizing the development of femininity, although the most common woman's role—*housewife*—demanded strenuous physical activity! Fortunately, the present trend is toward more activities for girls and women in the schools, as well as in careers, the occupational fields, politics, and community programs.

As an activity, track and field in and of itself cannot develop all the positive attributes needed by the female; but, it can provide an opportunity for a maximum expenditure of energy, which is what many women need today. It can provide physical, mental, and emotional development while not detracting from the female image. There is a need to interest more women in participating.

1

Track and field develops and helps to maintain the effective functioning of the heart and circulatory system, aids in relaxation and releasing nervous energy, improves digestion (probably by reducing tension), helps to control obesity, and improves the capacity of the respiratory system. It is valuable for all age groups, too.

Track and field activities are especially helpful in building endurance. Continuous participation increases respiratory rate and volume during an activity. Improvement is also shown in the circulatory system; the body has adequate circulation to remove the accumulated chemical substances that are formed during an activity. The number of capillaries increase and therefore enable more blood to be distributed to the working parts. The amount of oxygen which the blood is able to carry increases because there are more red blood corpuscles.

PARTICIPATION OUTSIDE OF CLASS

Track and field for women has become very popular. Most communities now have teams that practice under the leadership of qualified coaches.

The AAU Track and Field Rule Book[1] and DGWS Track and Field Guide Book[2] list the names and addresses of this sport's chairmen in various states. Write to these people for information about the nearest team or well-organized program in a specific locality. If none are available, a team or program may be started. There are girls who would like to participate, only they need to be asked. When a group of girls is willing to participate, one of the physical education teachers can be asked to coach or to assist in finding someone who is knowledgeable and willing to spend the time.

If a coach or other girls are not available, the coach of a local boys' team may allow a sincerely interested girl to work with his team and give the necessary assistance.

Competitive meets for girls and women in track and field are provided mainly by two organizations—the Division of Girls' and Women's Sports (DGWS) and the Amateur Athletic Union (AAU). Meets are conducted at the local, state, and national level. Each group has a national governing board that sets up the standards for girls and women participating in track and field.

Lesser competitive meets are conducted by youth agencies, schools, and church organizations for girls and women. If there is no such program, the feeling may be that the female is disinterested. One person can be instrumental in revealing this interest and in developing a program in track and field for girls and women.

Part I

TRACK EVENTS

The skills and events presented are starting, sprinting, middle-distance and distance running, high and low hurdles, and relay racing. Each chapter in this section covers the complete development of each event and skill. The grouping of these events is based on similarities in executing techniques.

The degree of perfecting techniques depends upon the goals of the participant. Basically, everyone knows how to run, for it is a speeded-up version of walking. However, the necessity to learn perfected movement patterns becomes paramount when athletes desire effective and efficient performances for given distances within set time variables.

Mamie Rallins, former world record holder in the 200-meter hurdles (World-Wide Photographers).

1

Starting

DESCRIPTION

Starting is the pivotal part of the race; it must be as smooth and rhythmical as any other movement in the race.

The basic concern is to reach top speed as quickly as possible. Acceleration must follow the initial thrust so closely that it becomes part of the same movement. Thus, when the gun is fired the function of starting blocks is to give maximum efficiency to the thrust of the first drive forward.

Fig. 1.1. Crouch Start. Take your mark (*a*), "set" (*b*), crouch start (*c*) (S. Lee Swaine)

Selection of Front and Back Legs

The first consideration in the *crouch start* is to use one of several methods to determine the front and back legs. A right-handed person usually places the left leg forward; a left-handed person, the right leg forward. The leg that is forward in the block has the sustained pushing force. The back leg must have maximum coordination and reflex action so that it may be brought through quickly for the first stride.

Exercises for Foot Selection
1. Stand with feet together and have a partner push from behind. The foot used to prevent falling forward is the back foot.
2. Starting with both feet together, step forward and kick an object. The foot selected to kick will be placed on the back block.

Block Spacing

Experiment must determine the ideal distance in block-spacing. Differences in height, leg length, and muscular development will necessitate whether the front block should be set back from the starting line anywhere from 12 to 20 inches. The space between the two blocks generally determines which type of start is to be used.

The Start

Three of the most universally used starts are

bunch

elongated

medium

Research has revealed the medium start to be the most effective[13]. It allows both legs to contribute powerfully to the initial drive and heightens the effectiveness of the front leg's final thrust to build up acceleration.

Commands

Three commands are given in the start: "Take your mark," "Set," and "Go." Each requires a change in body positions.

Fig. 1.2. Types of Starts. Bunch (*a*), medium (*b*), elongated (*c*) (S. Lee Swaine)

"Take your mark"

There are four points to remember when taking the stance for the start.

1. From a position well in front of the starting line, stoop down and walk backwards into the block, pressing both feet firmly against the blocks, just touching the ground. (See Fig. 1.3.)

2. Place hands behind the starting line exactly shoulder-width apart and support the body with the fingertips.

3. Straighten arms to keep shoulders high.

4. Balance the body between the hands and knee of the back leg, which is resting on the ground. Focus the eyes 3 to 5 inches in front of the line. The entire position should be one of comfort and alertness.

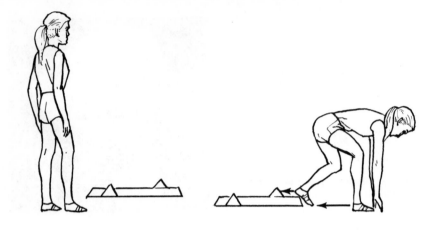

a

b

c

d

e

Fig. 1.3. **"Take Your Mark."** Before command (*a*), after command (*b*), waiting for next command (*c*), side view (*d*), front view (*e*)

Exercise for "Take Your Mark"
Assume the "Take your mark" position. Have a partner check the four points above. Also have her observe from the side and from behind to make certain that no body part is cramped.

"Set"

On the command "Set," all movements should be made slowly and deliberately so that the body's delicate poise is not disturbed. Hips are slightly higher if the blocks are closely spaced, and to the level of the shoulders if the blocks are farther apart. Body weight shifts forward 6 to 8 inches so that the shoulders extend to, or a few inches beyond, the starting line. At this point, arm and finger strength is crucial. Only those who have developed this strength can successfully execute the necessary body lean. Both arms remain quite straight, but elbows are not locked. Feet remain in firm contact with both blocks. The head is naturally aligned with the body—neither dropping below body level nor rising above it. (See Fig. 1.1.)

Exercise for "Set"
Move into the set position and hold for 2 seconds. Is there a feeling of instability? If so, do not be alarmed. Work on arm strength so that this position can be held. Have a partner check.

"Go"

Action immediately follows "Go," or the firing of the starting gun. Concentration and repeated practice are the only ways to cut down reaction time and achieve consistently good starts. *When the signal sounds, mind and body are tuned to instant response.* One arm is thrust forward as if about to shake hands; the other is thrust back. Arm movements should be just powerful enough to balance the actions of the legs; if exaggerated, they will upset the body's balance. The thrust of legs against the blocks occurs practically simultaneously. The back leg comes forward for the first stride; the front leg continues to push against the block until that leg is straight, thus providing maximum drive in propelling the body forward. Arm and leg motions follow each other within a split second and should allow the body to drive out of the blocks in a forward and upward movement. The body remains low for 10 to 15 yards.

Exercises for Learning Starting Technique
1. Take about six starts. Have a partner observe body positions. Run about 20 yards. Time both standing and crouch starts with

a stopwatch. If the crouch start is slower than the standing start, it is not being executed effectively. Recheck all points and repeat starts.

2. Use a barrier such as finish yarn. Line up across the track about 4 feet high and 3 yards from the starting line. On the signal "Go," a runner should be able to run underneath without touching the yarn. This is a good technique for developing low drive out of block.

Many beginners feel that they are losing their balance on the first few strides. This is frequently a good sign. To prevent falling, raise the knees higher and move arms and legs faster. Do not stop suddenly when practicing starts. Beyond the required distance, slow down gradually to a halt.

MECHANICAL PRINCIPLES OPERATIVE AT CRITICAL PARTS OF STARTING

The start begins from a position of relative instability, with the center of gravity just within the base in front of the forward foot. Since the runner must overcome inertia and great resistance during the first forward body movements, utmost power must be exerted in order for maximum acceleration on the signal "Go." Newton's third law states: *The force of the push, times the amount of time it acts, equals the momentum of the body.*

Exert pressure with both feet; the rear foot exerts the greater force because of the speed of movement. According to Henry,[13] the forward foot contributes twice as much to block velocity because its impulse has a longer duration.

In the set position, hips should be raised higher than shoulders in a forward direction to aid the degree of instability in the direction of intended force. Hips should not be so high that the rear leg is perfectly straight, however, for the sprinter would have to move her hips down before moving out of the starting blocks. This downward movement would dissipate the horizontal force and enhance gravity's pull on the body. The body should be driven from the blocks at an angle less than 45 degrees. This position allows the legs to extend with greater force and results in increased acceleration. Thus, Newton's second law: *The acceleration of a body is proportional to the force causing it.*

The angle of the start should be as far forward as can be controlled, with the runner concentrating on propelling the center of gravity in a straight line. If this straight line action is remembered, the runner should be falling with balance—that is, keeping her weight just so far forward that the up-driving knees and legs can partially but not quite catch balance.

Arm action is of great significance in overcoming inertia and in driving the body forward at the start and throughout the sprint. The left arm (assuming the right leg is back) is thrown straight ahead, only slightly bent at the elbow; the right arm moves straight back. If arms are chopped upward, they will most likely straighten the body.

COMMON ERRORS AND CORRECTIONS

Guessing at Foot Spacing

Once a successful starting position is attained, the same block spacing should be used consistently in relationship to the starting line. With feet, hands, or fingers, measure the distance of the front block from the starting line and the distance of the front and back blocks from the starting line. The runner must remember these measurements and set up her blocks in this manner each time.

Hips Too High

If a runner does not seem relaxed with hips at shoulder level, the blocks may be too close to the hands. Therefore, move both feet back a few inches. It should be understood that this is an immediate adjustment; the underlying problem is lack of shoulder and finger strength and must be resolved as quickly as possible. Use the applicable isometric exercises in Appendix G.

Hips Too Low

Move both feet closer to the line.

Off-Balance Forward

Shoulders probably extend too far ahead of hands. The runner should hold herself in the proper balanced position, taking more weight on the lead foot and less on the hands.

Too Far Back in Blocks

The runner should raise her hips and/or bring them forward, putting more weight on her hands.

Rear Leg Bent Too Much

Move the back block a few inches to the rear. Note that an acceptable method of starting, called the *medium high hip start,* is to bend the back leg slightly more than 140 degrees. If the back leg is too straight, move the block a few inches closer to the line.

Too Much Weight on Rear Leg

Adjust the front block until the front leg takes more weight than the rear leg.

Faults in Breathing

The runner should avoid excessive deep breaths. An optimum breathing pattern is learned by experience. Breathing should be natural and automatic between the signal "Set" and pistol shot.

Inattention

Attention to the starter is mandatory. Any action detracting from this is in error and must be avoided.

Too Tense on the Mark

Tension is partly caused by remaining too long in the crouch starting position. It can be avoided by slowly taking the mark position. No ribbons are given to the most obedient person who takes her mark first. Seen on television, it seems as if the world's greatest athletes are forever getting to their mark after the command is given!

False Start by an Opponent

On the starter's signal, "Everyone up," the runner won't merely stand up, but will run out of the block. This also provides extra practice at a start.

False Starts

The tendency to make false starts often originates at practice sessions. During practice, make certain that the start is held as faithfully as at a meet. The time between signals "Set" and "Go" should agree with official rules (approximately 2 seconds). Holding for shorter times during practice sessions makes it unlikely for the runner to wait out a slow starter. At the meet, the runner should take a few starts with the starter as he is starting other heats, thus familiarizing herself with the starter's techniques.

Falling Out of the Block

The runner should elongate the first step; coming out of the block, she may not be lifting her knees enough.

Straightening Up Too Soon

This is a common mistake with beginners. See that the first step is not too long, and make certain that the front foot pushes off that block until it is straight. This helps to keep the body in a more horizontal plane at ground contact. Refer to exercises related to this error in the description of starting.

TEACHING PROGRESSION

Teach or work on the following:

foot selection for forward and backward leg

foot spacing

"Take your mark" (body position)

"Set" (movement pattern and body position)

"Go" (movement pattern)

"Go" and movement patterns to the 20- and 25-yard marks

RULES

- Hands must be on the ground and behind the line (not on the line).
- Both feet must be behind the starting line, with part of each foot in contact with the ground. This means that the toes of both feet must be in contact with the ground even though a starting block is used.

- The signal "Set" must not be given until each girl is motionless at the lines.
- After the signal "Set," no one may move until the signal "Go."
- There is no penalty for one false start. A runner is disqualified after two false starts.

2

Sprinting

DESCRIPTION

Sprints are races that are run from start to finish at full speed. In Olympic competition these events are the 100 and 200-meter dashes.

Fig. 2.1. **Chi Cheng** setting a new world record in the 100-yard dash at the national outdoor AAU championships. Note her excellent upright, relaxed driving form and high knee action (World-Wide Photographers).

Nationally, distances are run in either meters or yards. Locally, and for national girls (aged 14 to 17), sprinting races are 50, 60, and 75 yards. Actually, any race up to 200 meters (220 yards) is considered a sprint for the female.

There are two methods of getting from one place to another faster than an opponent.

1. Move the legs faster.

2. Have a longer stride and one that carries the runner low to the ground.

These statements apply in running events where fatigue is not an element. The length of the stride is of paramount importance in sprinting. An example:

Runner A has faster leg movements; Runner B has a stride 8 inches longer than A. Therefore, each time B puts her foot down she gains 8 inches; in 50 steps she gains 11 additional yards.

There is not much a coach can do about leg speed except to eliminate wasted incorrect movements that cause inefficient and ineffective patterns. The runner must work toward developing the most efficient stride—a long, low one.

Good Sprint Form

The following are not natural, so they must be practiced:

high knee action

good foreleg reach

landing high on toes

good arm action

bouncing forward, not up

good forward lean (20 degrees)

running tall, with back straight

relaxation (loose hands and loose neck and face muscles)

Fig. 2.2.   Exaggerated Knee Lift

Leg Action

High Knee Action

All running should be performed with knees high, and the runner should land high on her toes. Knees must be lifted high to obtain maximum power from the thighs and legs. When told to lift her knees, a beginner lifts the foreleg behind, almost hitting her buttock. This action is incorrect and should be avoided, particularly in the early stages of learning; it should not be confused with high knee action.

Exercise for High Knee and Proper Leg Action
1. Raise alternate knees while standing in place. Touch hands to knees, palms down at navel level.
2. Same method as 1 above, but run in place.
3. Lift knees high and run about 20 yards down a grassy area or the track infield. Stay high on toes.

Foreleg Reach

When done correctly, this technique can make the difference between a champion and a good sprinter. It is an advanced move-

Fig. 2.3.   Foreleg Reach Exercise

ment that should be carefully and diligently practiced by top sprinters rather than beginners. The coach should decide whether to emphasize it or not; if poorly done, it could lessen the force of leg thrust, thereby reducing speed. Swing the foreleg forward while lifting the knee. From this position, bring the foot down to the ground and touch high on the toes.

Exercises for Foreleg Reach
1. Walk, attempting to throw the hip and knee forward at the same time. Walk slowly and concentrate on this new and different technique. It is necessary to relax—simultaneously thrusting hip and knee will cause the foreleg to reach in front. If concentration on foreleg reach is too great, it resembles a drum majorette's strut rather than the desired pattern. Until the runner develops a kinesthetic feel for this technique, running with foreleg reach is not encouraged.
2. Run slowly on the grass, exaggerating the reach of the foreleg several times. Take wind sprints, using the foreleg reach technique. See Appendix I.

Fig. 2.4.   Arm Action Exercise

Arm Action

Elbows should be bent at a 90-to-95-degree angle and arms should hang freely from the shoulders. All arm action should be forward and backward. On the forward thrust the hand should not be raised higher than the shoulders; on the backward thrust the wrist should not pass behind or below the hips. Arm action coordinates with leg action, arms always move as fast as the legs. If the foreleg reach technique is used, arms swing on the forward thrust no higher than the bust and no further back than the hip.

Exercises for Arm Action
1. Let arms hang naturally at sides — with hands half open, slightly cupped, and relaxed. Bend arms at elbow until they are level with hips, hands still and relaxed. Keeping arms bent, pump them backward and forward. Drive from elbows and shoulders, not wrist. The faster the arms move, the faster the sprinter goes; therefore, develop the ability to pump the arm vigorously to get additional speed.
2. Stand in place and move the arms correctly. A partner should observe side, front, and rear. Walk, then run 20 to 30 yards. Raise knees properly while moving arms as fast as legs.
3. Run with partner, maintaining an even and low stride. Now, *without trying to go faster,* exaggerate one runner's arm reach. Note that the person who has exaggerated the arm reach will pull

away without extra effort. (Be sure to keep arms low and reach forward.)

Body Lean and Posture

Eyes should be focused approximately 20 yards on the ground in front of the sprinter. This prevents the head from being held either too high or too low and will inhibit head movement. It also helps to eliminate undue body lean or inefficient body straightness. Body lean should be approximately 20 to 30 degrees.

Give careful consideration to a tall running appearance, rather than leaning only at the waist or "sitting down" in the run. (The latter is demonstrated by protruding buttocks.) The running action should be forward rather than up and down. "Up and down" running usually indicates that a runner has both feet simultaneously off the ground. This only minimizes the force and power necessary for maximum performance, for a body free in air cannot exert maximum force.

Exercises for Body Lean and Sprinting Posture
1. Starting with feet together, lean forward from the heels about 30 degrees from vertical. Maintaining this angle, stride down the field with eyes focused 20 yards ahead. Repeat several times.
2. To practice running tall, put hands against the wall and back up as far as possible with heels on the ground. Then rise on toes, lift lead knee, and *feel* the power. (For contrast, stick out buttocks and note how much power is lost.)
3. Place a string vertically and head high across the running area. The runner runs forward. Observe her head; it should not move above the string but should maintain a straight line as the runner proceeds forward.
4. To develop ankle bounce, lock knees and bound forward, just flipping the ankles. When the runner tires, she may walk. Repeat: Walk, bound, walk.

Relaxation

The consistent winner has mastered all techniques previously mentioned plus the art of relaxing. In competitions, a sprinter will be confronted with many runners of equal speed or better. To win the important races it is necessary to remain relaxed while the other runners are tensing up. Relaxation can be taught only during practice. If never practiced, the words from the coach, *"Relax—you*

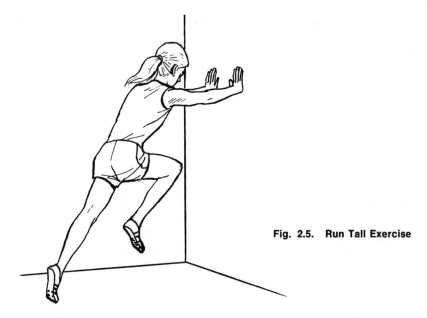

Fig. 2.5.   Run Tall Exercise

are too tense," will mean absolutely nothing at race time. No one has ever increased speed by tightening facial muscles, bunching shoulders, or fighting like mad!

Exercises for Relaxation
1. When running wind sprints, use nine-tenths maximum effort rather than full speed. Top speed is not necessary in all practice sessions.
2. Practice running with exaggeratedly loose jaws and hands.

MECHANICAL PRINCIPLES OPERATIVE AT CRITICAL PARTS OF SPRINTING

Running movement is efficient only when the athlete is maintaining proper balance. Balance depends considerably on correct angling of the trunk and on arm movement in the direction of the run. The body is propelled forward by the push backward against the ground, equal to the force applied as the foot makes contact with the ground. *For balanced running, the movements of the vertical and horizontal force components of drive must be equal at the runner's center of gravity.*

To avoid toppling forward as the race progresses, the runner must assume a more erect position. This in turn diminishes the amount of power one can apply because the horizontal component of force is reduced.

The head, by virtue of its weight and position on the spine, can have considerable effect on other parts of the body. Consequently, its carriage is of utmost importance. The head should be maintained in a natural alignment with the shoulders, eyes focused about 20 yards straight down the track. Eye focus at this distance will tend to correct the head position.

Running speed is the product of both length and frequency of stride. Maximum efficiency can be attained only when they are in correct proportion to each other—depending mainly on the runner's height, build, strength, flexibility, and coordination.

Many coaches do not emphasize the importance of the impetus afforded by foot pushing; instead, they continue to concentrate on the concept of pulling. The quick forward movement of the body is a result of the vertical and horizontal components of force pushing behind the body's center of gravity; it is not caused by a pulling motion. This concept of momentum from pushing is an application of Newton's third law: *"For every action there is always an equal and opposite reaction."*

Although fast running requires a long stride, for efficient running the lead foot is never stretched awkwardly to lengthen the stride. Stride length results from driving the entire body forward and depends upon strong abdominal muscles and high knee action.

One of the most important considerations has not been mentioned: relaxing those muscles not directly involved, and exerting force that will propel the body forward with the least possible expenditure of energy but maximum force of movement. *The faster the speed of the run, the longer the stride; the longer the run, the shorter the stride.* Legs should move in a manner that enables the center of gravity to move forward with as little retardation as possible, while still exerting the correct force for the race.

COMMON ERRORS AND CORRECTIONS

Arm Action

Arms should carry across the body rather than forward and back. This fault tends to throw the entire action off balance. Arm action usually relates to leg action. Emphasize that all action must be as "straight ahead" as possible. Make sure arm action is vigorous.

Tenseness

Watch for tightly clenched fists and taut forearm muscles. Are jaws tight? These indicate a lack of relaxation. Follow the exercises related to relaxation. Check for erectness of head and neck, as this tenses back muscles. The runner should always look 20 yards ahead to eliminate head erectness.

Improper Body Lean

To gain a lean, be careful that the legs aren't "left behind." Knees must stay forward under the lean, as they lose all effectiveness in a kickup behind. Be certain also that the lean is not all above the waist. Usually this is most evident in the first 10 to 20 yards. Paying attention to start and high knee lift will help to eliminate this fault. Faulty lean, not unlike poor arm action, is a symptom and not a cause. Correction of the knee lift will probably correct any faults with the lean.

Quitting Before the Finish

The runner should think of the finish line as being 5 to 10 yards beyond; any slowing up will take place after the line is passed. Follow this technique faithfully in practice, for slowing up before the finish line is a difficult habit to break. Is it caused by fatigue or, simply, sloppy practice habits? In the 220-yard dash it is frequently a problem of fatigue, which results from the distance. Therefore, 330-yard dashes are a must at practice. (Refer to the training schedule in Appendix I.)

Excessive Body Movements

Moving the head to observe an opponent slows down running efficiency. The runner should observe through peripheral vision only; all else is unimportant. This error may be corrected by

constant awareness and attempts to improve

working on running form at less than full speed, particularly during wind sprints (see training schedule in Appendix I for a description of wind sprints)

TEACHING PROGRESSIONS

Teach or work on the following:

leg action
  knee lift
  foreleg reach
  forward and low bound

arm action

torso position
  body angle (lean)
  head and eye focus
  upright as opposed to "sitting" posture

RULES

- Runners must remain in lane throughout race.

- On a straightaway the choice of lanes is determined by fastest times for the semifinal and final races. The center lane is awarded to the runner with the fastest time. The next fastest runner is in the lane to her right, the third fastest in the lane to her left. The selection continues from right to left until all lanes are filled; the two slowest runners are in lanes 1 and 8. Under some rules, runners on a curve are placed in lanes 1 through 8 according to times; according to other rules, all contestants draw for lanes in any race run on a curve.

- A runner may not be materially aided by a coach, teammates, or mechanical device.

- A runner places at the finish line in the order in which any part of her torso reaches the finish line. A runner who falls has not finished the race unless and until her entire body has crossed the line.

STRATEGY

Chapter 13 discusses fundamental strategy in preparing for a meet. The intent here is to identify the strategy that is often utilized by the champion in her specialized event. The champion does not always distinguish herself because her skills are better than her competitors, but because she has developed the capacity to tolerate heavier loads. Each person has a *physiological limit* (the point beyond which she cannot perform without injury) and a *psychological limit* (the point at which she tells herself she is too tired to go any further). In maximum performance, the trick is to move the psychological limit as close as possible to the physiological limit. This is exactly what a champion does. The gap between the two is not suddenly narrowed during competition, but has been developed gradually during the training season.

In sprints, the major requisite is speed; but the following tips will enhance general performance.

Become familiar with the starter. Move blocks off to the side so that his commands can be heard. Take practice starts with the starter, noting his inflections and the length of time he holds the runners in the *set* position.

Warm up before each event. One warm-up will not suffice if there is a time span between events. Proper warm-up will also lessen the chance of injury.

Wear a light-colored top. Since many races are close, a light-colored top will enable the judge to see the runner and perhaps select her as a qualifier.

Unless the lean has been mastered, run through the finish line (5 to 10 yards beyond). Do not slow down.

3

Middle-Distance Running

DESCRIPTION

The technique of the middle-distance runner (quarter and half-miler) differs slightly from that of sprinters. The form is less difficult to execute than sprinting. The greatest difficulty comes with insufficient conditioning to develop cardiorespiratory endurance, or stamina, and muscular strength. Both are needed to maintain speed over the great distances in these races.

Fig. 3.1. Sprinter's Knee Lift (a). Chi Cheng, world record holder in both the 100-yard dash and the 200-meter dash. **Middle Distancer's Knee Lift** (b). First lap of an 880-yard race at the 1970 National AAU Championships; Sandra Toussaint (third position) goes forward to win this event (World-Wide Photographers).

The middle-distance runner's stride is shorter than the sprinter's, yet longer than the distance runner's, and must be developed by experimentation. There is less body lean and lower knee action than in sprinting, and a higher back kick than in distance running. Arms, in a relaxed position, are carried at about waist height. The action of the foot plant is on the balls of the feet rather than high on the toes as in sprinting.

Races beyond and including the mile require a distinct form that is different from that of the sprinter, middle-distance half-miler, or quarter-miler. One fault of many middle-distance women is that they emulate distance running form. Consequently, they are less able to do what the middle-distance race requires—sprint for position, settle down into a relaxed stride for pacing, sustain an extended drive for the tape.

Drill for Middle-Distance Running Technique
Sprint 100 yards. Run the same distance, but do not raise knees too high. Lower arms, and do not lean as much. Stride lengths should be slightly shorter. Do you feel the difference? Are you relaxed? Alternate 6 to 8 times between sprinting and middle-distance forms at 40 yards each.

MECHANICAL PRINCIPLES

Mechanical principles do not differ greatly from those of sprinting and, therefore, are not included in this section. Refer to Chapter 2, "Sprinting," if this information is desired. See also Chapter 4, "Cross Country."

COMMON ERRORS AND CORRECTIONS

Since middle-distance running technique does not differ greatly from that of sprinting, the section Common Errors and Corrections for sprinters (Chapter 2) would be applicable to middle-distance runners.

TEACHING PROGRESSION

Teach or work on the following:

conditioning

curve running

pacing (ability to run a specific time for critical parts of the race)

strategy

RULES

- Hands and feet behind starting line.
- Two false starts disqualify a runner.
- The direction of the run is counterclockwise. In the 220-yard and quarter-mile race, the runner begins with a staggered start and remains in her lane throughout the race.
- In the 880-yard and mile race, the runner breaks for the pole lane (first lane) after completing the first turn.
- A runner places at the finish line in the order in which any part of her torso reaches the line. A runner who falls has not completed the race unless and until her entire body has crossed the line.

STRATEGY

For fundamental strategy in preparing for a meet, see Chapter 13. In this section the intent is to identify the strategy often used by the champion in middle-distance running.

If an opponent has great strength but little speed, let her set the pace; then, outsprint her at the end.

If she has great speed but little strength, set the pace. At the distance at which she plans to sprint, make certain the opponent is too far behind to catch up.

If an opponent has both strength and speed, plan the race according to your own capacity and run according to that plan.

Passing to take the lead must have a purpose. Either the pace is too slow or the runner is nearing the tape. When passing, try to catch the opponent by surprise so that she does not have time to contest the pass. Once the pass is made, use the extra momentum to build up the distance between you and the opponent.

To prevent a pass, run wide on the curves (but not wide enough to allow an opponent to sneak in on the inside). Contest an attempted pass, thereby forcing the opponent to expend energy. Hold off the pass as long as possible on the straightaway, for it is easier to prevent passing on the curve.

Run at the right shoulder of an opponent, not directly behind her, to avoid being boxed in. A third person might move up to her right shoulder, and you would then be boxed in between the two of them.

The quarter-mile race is considered a sprint event, beginning with a staggered start and continuing in the lanes throughout. Run the curves closer to the inside of your lane, as this slightly lessens the distance to be run.

If the turn is sharp, lean toward the pole by lowering the left shoulder and arm and planting the right leg slightly over the left.

If the race is run on a curve, the start is staggered and run in lanes throughout the race, start in the lane behind your opponent. During competition this will allow a full view of the field of runners while making a move on the lead.

Never let the leaders build up a huge margin; rarely can one catch up.

Conserve energy and do not make foolish challenges too early in the race. Middle-distance races require more strategy than the other running events for women.

4

Cross-Country Running

DESCRIPTION

In cross-country running, the emphasis is on endurance rather than on great speed and a long stride. The distance runner's knee action is much lower than that of the sprinter, and slightly lower than that of the middle-distance runner. Thus, the low knee action results in a short stride and less speed. And, the less energy expended, the longer the runner can endure without tiring.

Arms swing freely from the shoulders in a forward and backward motion, at the same speed as the legs. Hands swing no higher than the shoulders on the forward thrust and no farther back than the hip on the backswing. Fingers are flexed and the fist is relaxed—not tightly clenched.

Head position is controlled by eye contact. Looking at the ground approximately 30 yards ahead will provide the proper head position. It should also provide the slight body lean that is preferred to the upright running position and/or the greater lean used by the sprinter. Good distance runners do not land heel first. They land low on the balls of the feet, drop down on the heel, then push off with the toes. This is called a *ball-heel-ball* action. Back kick (how high the heels are kicked toward the buttocks) need not be a concern, since the correct position will be a natural result of the low knee action.

Much preparation is needed to run a race of 2 miles or more. For beginners, a lesser load should be attempted, then gradually increased.

Exercises for Distance Running Techniques

1. Do not use a sprinter's track shoe; select a running shoe without spikes that has a heel. Run several 120-yard windsprints at about half of maximum speed. Concentrate on executing the techniques of distance running form described above. Have a partner evaluate form.

2. Start with 5 minutes of running in a given direction without stopping each day, until you feel comfortable and there is little fatigue. Then increase the schedule to 8 minutes. If planning to compete, increase the time of the run by 3 minutes, until you can run up to a half hour or hour. (If not, set a goal involving less time.) Each time the schedule changes, select a different setting for the run.

Running Downhill on Uneven Terrain

Much cross-country running involves traversing uneven terrain, from slight inclines to steep hills. When running downhill, the pull of gravity works to one's advantage, as the slope pulls the body forward. In these instances, the stride should be shortened to ensure proper footing; the body should remain relaxed and the run controlled. To prevent undue imbalance, the center of gravity should remain over the base of support.

Exercise for Running Downhill
Select a steep hill. Walk to the top and run to the bottom. Relax and let gravity do the work. Try it again, only this time fight the pull of gravity by slowing up and leaning back; this prevents a faster descent. Note that this latter technique can be used if the incline is too steep. Now repeat running downhill several times, using the pull of gravity to advantage.

Running Uphill on Uneven Terrain

Running uphill is a greater challenge than running downhill. The runner must lean forward, lift knees higher, lengthen the stride, and swing the arms harder. When nearing an incline, she must run to the top, increasing speed about 5 yards before the incline to help build up the momentum needed to mount the hill.

Exercise for Running Uphill
Move at least 10 yards back from the hill. Start running, picking up the pace at least 5 yards before the incline. Try to remain relaxed

Fig. 4.1. Distance Runner's Form. Frances Larrieu, winner of the 1500-meter run at the Women's National AAU Outdoor Championships, has relaxed arm carry. This is the last lap of the 1500-meter run; in *a, b, c,* and *d,* note her good knee action. Most runners at this stage of the race find it difficult to lift their knees high enough to maintain

the desired speed. Because of fatigue, runners are also very tense at this point. Miss Larrieu does not evince these errors. She obviously has the endurance to push toward national championships (World-Wide Photographers).

while running uphill. Concentrate on a high knee lift and an increased length of stride. Focus eyes about 15 yards ahead. Avoid looking at the top of the hill, as this causes the body to straighten and throws the center of gravity behind the base of support and creates an imbalance.

Sore thighs and calves are likely to result if the two preceding learning experiences are attempted without preparation. Continue to exercise the same muscles at future workouts. Heat applications are beneficial between workouts. Each workout, including the running of hills, ought to be incorporated into a longer run. If possible, the terrain should include hills that are spaced sufficiently apart to allow a degree of rest between each one.

MECHANICAL PRINCIPLES OPERATIVE AT CRITICAL PARTS OF DISTANCE RUNNING

Force cannot be applied unless there is an equal and opposite counter force. A body free in air has no force against which it can react. (Newton's third law) There is a period when both feet are off the ground, but a secret of successful cross-country running is to minimize this period of nonsupport. The power for forward motion is supplied by the *extensors* of the driving leg—that is, the extending rear leg. The force of the action—reaction of the foot against the ground—produces a longer stride and, hence, the period of nonsupport. Thus, by shortening the length of the stride, the period of nonsupport can be reduced. (This principle has been used by male European runners.) A short stride keeps the period of nonsupport to a minimum and prevents the center of gravity from rising and falling as much as it would with the middle-distance runner's longer stride.

If the center of gravity is behind the vertical, greater force will be needed for forward movement. The body leans approximately 20 degrees, thereby maintaining the center of gravity over the striding leg as it contacts the ground. If the angle is not great enough, the center of gravity will not be forward when the lead foot hits the ground.

Added force may be obtained by using the muscle force of more joints. More forceful contraction can be obtained by putting muscles under stretch. Knee slightly bent, the runner lands low on the ball of her foot. The heel then eases to the ground. This movement also allows the gastrocnemius[1] to stretch before contracting.

For every action there is an equal and opposite reaction. At one time, coaches advocated a high rear-heel action of the leg position in recovery. Now runners are encouraged to use a lower kickup with a less forceful thrust exerted by the extending leg, coupled with a shorter stride.

Reaction to angular movement in athletics is balanced by rotation in the opposite direction. Arms should be carried low with a bend at the elbow greater than 90 degrees. Arm action coordinates with leg action. If the knees are not lifted high, the angle of the arm bend will be proportionately shallow.

COMMON ERRORS AND CORRECTIONS

Staying Off the Ground Too Long

Avoid overstriding. Shortening the stride will keep the center of gravity from rising and falling dramatically and will keep the period of nonsupport at a minimum.

Losing Balance While Going Up a Steep Hill

Avoid looking too far ahead toward the top of the hill, and attempt to keep the center of gravity forward in the direction of the run.

Losing Balance While Running Down a Steep Hill

Aim to keep the center of gravity within the base of support.

High Knee Action

Since it creates fatigue, avoid high knee action in long distances.

Tenseness

Relax arms and do not clench fists. Jaws and wrists should be loose.

---

[1] The gastrocnemius is the largest and most superficial muscle of the calf of the leg.

TEACHING PROGRESSION

Teach or work on the following:

> running techniques (5-minute runs)
>
> stamina (increase either distance or time at each practice session)
>
> pacing
>
> familiarity with different terrains

RULES

- Maximum distance for women in competition is 2 miles.
- Eight females compose a team.
- Scoring is computed by counting the number of points credited to the first five members finishing from each team. One point is given for first, two for second, and so on through the fifth member of each team. The team with the *lowest* number of points is declared the winner.

STRATEGY

The secret of distance running is "pace," or the proper distribution of energy over the distance to be covered. The runner's first concern should be an even pace throughout the race, and she should simply put all her energy into the finishing sprint when nearing the end of the race. A person with strength and pace knowledge can often take the speed out of a "kicker" during the body of a race.

Racing tactics in a long-distance run are less important than those in a shorter race because after a few hundred yards the field is usually not bunched, and, there is more time to recover from errors made during shorter races. Alertness is vital. Pace and position must be maintained.

5

Relay Racing

DESCRIPTION

A relay team composed of good sprinters can lose to a slower team that has superior ability in baton exchange. The pursuit relay is the most popular and involves distances of 220 yards to a mile. The distances denote the total distance the four runners cover. The official national and international relays are:

quarter-mile (4 x 110)

half-mile (4 x 220)

mile (4 x 440)

The medley[1] relay of 110, 110, 220, and 440 is an official half-mile relay.

Successful relay racing hinges on baton passing. Three methods are commonly employed in baton exchange.

1. *Conventional nonvisual pass:* The baton is transferred from the incoming runner's left hand to the receiver's right hand. This is the most widely used exchange.

2. *Sprint pass:* The baton is passed from the passer's left to the receiver's right hand (first exchange), from the passer's right to receiver's left (second exchange), left to right (third exchange). The receiver does not transfer the baton to her other hand.

[1]"Medley" indicates that the four runners do not run the same distance.

3. *Visual pass:* The baton is carried in the first runner's right hand and passed to the receiver's left hand. The receiver then transfers the baton to her right hand. This method is good when lanes are not provided and when speed of movement to the inside position is imperative.

CONVENTIONAL NONVISUAL PASS

The success of the exchange depends upon the coordination between incoming runner and receiver. It is the receiver's responsibility to provide the incoming runner with a good target for placing the baton. The target area is between the forefinger and thumb. The receiver's shoulders and hips face the direction of the run, and eyes focus ahead. The right arm is extended at the side of the body, with fingers together pointing toward the ground. The palm faces the passer, and the thumb is well away from the fingers (about 3 inches from the body). As the baton snaps into the pocket between the fingers and the thumb, the hand closes and securely holds the baton. Then, transfer the baton to the left hand so that it can be passed. This transfer takes place in a rhythmical fashion, as close as possible to the natural arm swing.

Passer and receiver should stagger themselves so that the passer's left shoulder could bump the receiver's right shoulder. This, of course, should never happen. As the passer approaches, she watches the target of the receiver and must not attempt to pass until the pocket is provided. When the target is provided, from a natural arm swing, the passer's arm straightens and is brought forward toward the receiver's hand. The passer's wrist vigorously flexes upward to snap the baton in the pocket. (See Fig. 5.1.)

Exercises for Passing and Receiving
1. Four runners, facing the same direction, line up a yard apart behind each other. Numbers 2, 3, and 4 put hands back to receive. Number 1 steps forward and snaps the baton into 2's right hand; 2 transfers the baton to her left hand and passes to 3. When the fourth girl receives the baton, all do an about-face. Number 4 is now Number 1. Repeat several times. Someone should observe body positions and exchange from the side.
2. Spread out so that there is enough distance between each girl to walk. Go through the above exercise.

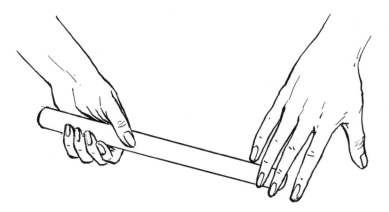

Fig. 5.1.   Baton Exchange. Conventional (*a*), nonvisual (*b*)

The preceding drills are primarily for learning the fundamental techniques of passing and receiving. In actuality, both passer and receiver run at top speed. Speed must not decrease when making the exchange.

Fig. 5.2. Conventional Nonvisual Exchange. Receiving in the left hand, *a*, passing with the right hand, *b*. The 400-meter relay, taken at a National AAU Women's Championship Meet (World-Wide Photographers).

Passing and Receiving in the Exchange Zone

The baton must pass from one sprinter to another within a 22-yard passing zone. An 11-yard marker stands before and beyond each 110-yard point of the 440-yard relay; these mark the 22-yard exchange zone. A restraining line is provided 11 yards before the beginning of each passing (or exchange) zone. The receiver may start on this restraining line so that she has a greater distance in which to build up momentum. Passing can take place only within the exchange zone, preferably within the last 15 to 18 yards, as illustrated in Fig. 5.2.

Drills for Exchange Zone Technique

1. *Establishing the checkmark.* Set up a passing zone (Fig. 5.3) to establish a checkmark for the receiver. From the restraining line the receiver takes five big steps in the direction of the on-coming runner and marks this spot. Looking over her right shoulder and with minimum body turn, she returns to the restraining line and watches the oncoming runner. When the runner hits the checkmark, the receiver takes off with maximum speed. She places her hand in the receiving position about 5 yards before the end of the exchange zone. The runner should instantly snap the baton into the target. If the baton is not received in the zone, it has been done incorrectly. Determine whether the receiver should have started sooner or later, and move the checkmark accordingly.

Fig. 5.3. Passing Zone and Checkmarks

2. *Relay racing.* Determine the runners' positions and set up passing zones around a 440-yard track. Place a suitable object at both zone ends so that an observer can watch from the center. She should observe as many parts of the exchange as possible. Repeat this drill several times if you wish, but change the positions of runners; have them avoid fatigue by jogging about 80 yards, then sprint toward the exchange zones at maximum speed.

3. *Conditioning.* Use five people in relay racing. Place four at equal intervals around the track. The fifth person starts running and hands the baton to one of the waiting four, who runs to the next and hands off. At the spot where she handed off, each girl then waits for the baton to come around again. The drill can be carried on as many times as needed.

SPRINT PASS

In the relay sprint pass, the receiver does not transfer the baton to her other hand. This relay is frequently run by four girls who always run the same positions. (Although USA Women's Olympic Champion-

Fig. 5.4. Position of Receiver's Hand During Sprint Pass Baton Exchange

ship teams have used the conventional relay pass (switching from right hand to left, the author believes that a pass which does not require a switch to the nonreceiving hand could give a split-second time advantage.)

The first runner holds the baton in her left hand and, with a downward motion (Fig. 4.1, page 34), passes to the second runner's right hand. The baton passes from the third runner's right hand to her left hand. The third runner passes to the fourth runner's right hand, and the receiver holds her palm outstretched. The baton is brought down across her hand.

All other points related to the conventional baton exchange hold true; however, runners must be placed to the best advantage around the track because of the alternation in receiving hands. The second and fourth girls should be closer to the inside line; the third runner should receive toward the outside of the lane.

The same drills as those suggested in the previous sections can be used for the sprint pass exchange, except that receivers should be staggered in a checkerboard formation (Fig. 5.5).

VISUAL PASS

The visual pass is generally used in long-distance relays such as mile races. As indicated by its name, the outgoing runner watches the incoming runner in executing this pass. The receiver looks over her shoulder and down her extended right arm at the baton, at the same time keeping her hips straight forward in the lane. Only the head and upper portion of the body are turned, so that she can turn her head and shoulders and continue running in a straight line rather than laterally as soon as she has the baton.

When the oncoming runner is getting close to the receiver, she leans her body forward and extends her left arm with the baton. When within her grasp, the receiver circles her fingers around the top half of the baton and holds it firmly between her thumb and forefinger. She then transfers the baton from her right hand to her left during the first two steps, and does not interrupt the natural pumping action of her arms.

In passing and receiving the baton, the passer and receiver must work together to achieve a smooth yet rapid exchange. It is the receiver's responsibility to watch the oncoming runner and decide the passer's condition, since the receiver must determine when she should start running in order to be at a good pace when the exchange

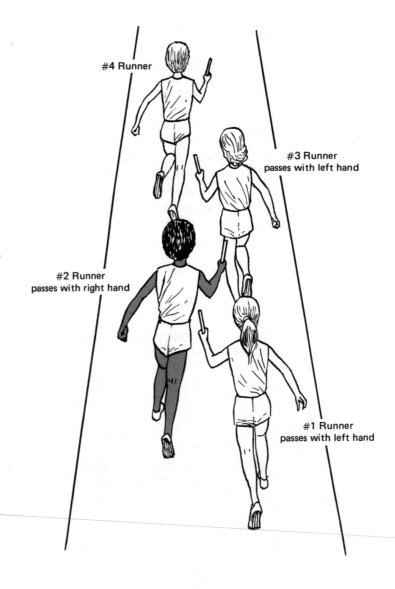

#4 Runner

#3 Runner
passes with left hand

#2 Runner
passes with right hand

#1 Runner
passes with left hand

Fig. 5.5.   Staggering Positions in Sprint Pass

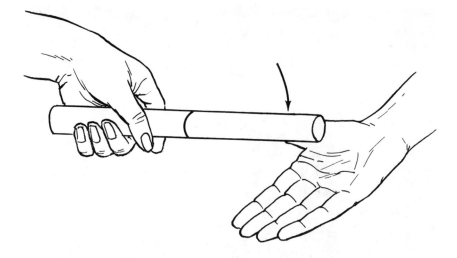

Fig. 5.6.   Visual Pass. Passer's and receiver's hand position

is made. If the passer is very tired, the receiver starts to run when the passer almost reaches her. If the passer is keeping a rapid pace, the receiver starts sooner to build momentum. At any rate, the incoming and outgoing runners should be running at the same pace when exchanging the baton. It is the passer's responsibility to keep her pace even when the receiver starts running, and to extend her arm and baton about a body's length before she reaches the receiver; this gives the receiver something to focus on before she grasps the baton.

Since the exchange is made from the passer's left hand to the receiver's right hand, the passer should run on the right side of the lane—and the receiver on the left side—to avoid a collision. Of course, the passer should never run into the receiver, as this would indicate that the receiver did not judge accurately the speed of the incoming runner.

COMMON ERRORS AND CORRECTIONS

Cocking the Baton

Cocking the baton is an error that can cause the passer to lose reaching contact-distance with the receiver. It is caused when the baton is held back behind the hips (similar to the backswing in a

Fig. 5.7. Visual Baton Exchange. These photos were taken of the mile relay (4 x 440) at a National AAU Championship Meet. *Note:* The receiver (*a, b, c*) keeps the passer in sight, judging her degree of fatigue or strength. Also note how close the runner is

before the receiver takes off. Because the passer has run a 440, the receiver who is fresh receives the baton after only 3 yards from the beginning of the passing zone (World-Wide Photographers).

racket sport) before it is snapped into the target. The baton pass should be a movement from the *hip forward*. The last movement is not an entire arm action, rather a flick of the wrist which snaps the baton into the target.

Passing the Baton with the Entire Arm

Not unlike cocking the baton, this is an error that slows up the pass and might cause the passer to lose reaching contact-distance with the receiver. It can be corrected in the same manner as cocking the baton.

Incomplete Baton Pass

An incomplete baton pass may be the result of many factors.

Lack of Proper Conditioning

Often a pass cannot be completed because the passer runs out of steam before she can catch the receiver. The correction is obvious. More conditioning is necessary—that is, more repetitions of running a distance greater than that required in the relay. Until this correction is made, the receiver should decrease the number of steps between checkmark and exchange.

Receiver Takes Off Too Soon

The passer is unable to catch the receiver in the allotted 20 yards, which will cause the entire relay to be disqualified. Hence, this error must be avoided. The passer should not yell, "Go," to the receiver, because in the heat of competition the receiver frequently cannot hear the command or the passer forgets to yell. Continuous practice must be provided, and the receiver must watch the correct checkmark and take off only when the passer hits that mark.

Insufficient Exposure of Baton

The passer should grip the baton close to its end so that most of its entire length is available to the receiver's grip.

Passer Slows Up When Approaching Receiver

This error can be serious, for it also slows down the speed of baton transfer. A valuable tenth of a second may be lost, or a pass missed if the cause, rather than the result, is not corrected. Usually the receiver has taken off too slowly and the passer has had to slow down to avoid overrunning her. Work with the receiver to ensure that she takes off at the proper time, and be sure she is using the correct number of steps for her takeoff mark. Is the receiver taking off with a sprinter's push-off and pumping both arms to build up maximum speed before putting her arm back to accept the baton?

Passer May Not Fully Extend

Frequently, a pass could have been completed if the passer had really extended or fully reached. Instill the idea in the passer's mind that she *must get the baton to the receiver,* and that the extension must be made at the same moment of passing the baton. An extension prior to this will slow down the passer and magnify the distance between the two.

Dropping the Baton

Dropping the baton may be the result of many factors.

Receiver Moving Her Hand

Once the hand is placed to receive the baton, it must remain in that position until the baton has been passed. A still target is easier to hit than a moving one.

Passer Not Watching the Target

The passer must keep her eyes on the target until the baton is released. Too often a passer sees the hand and then looks upward while passing the baton; the receiver moves her hand slightly, and the baton is dropped. Emphasize the importance of eyes on the target.

Bumping the Receiver

This is caused when the receiver takes off too soon or if an inadequate number of steps have been allotted for the checkmark. Runners at the same speed are usually allowed 5 strides. A slower runner can be given less, a faster runner more. Many national and international relay runners give the incoming runner 3 strides, but it must be remembered that these are perfect takeoffs in which there is not the slightest hesitation.

Pressure in Passing the Baton

The *snap* of the baton must be forceful enough for the receiver to know it has been passed. With enough pressure, this definite snap will cause a reflex action of closing the fingers around the baton.

Failure to Judge Speed

Judging the incoming runner's speed is most important in races where the distance is great enough to tire the incoming runner. The receiver must be able to judge the passer's fitness to run the given distance of the passing zone and make the necessary adjustments to receive the baton before fatigue slows her down.

Target Too Small

If, in the conventional pass, the receiver does not spread her thumb wide enough apart from the fingers, the target will be too small and the chance of the passer connecting will be minimized.

TEACHING PROGRESSION

Teach or work on the following:

passing and receiving from stationary position

passing and receiving while walking

passing and receiving while jogging

passing and receiving in exchange zone

passing and receiving in exchange zone at full speed

running at full speed through entire relay

RULES

- Four runners compose a relay. Each leg of the relay must run in the designated lane unless other rules are stated.
- A runner may run no more than one leg of a relay.
- During the exchange, the passer must pick up a dropped baton. *Outside the zone,* the baton is picked up by the runner who dropped it.

- An extension line is placed 11 yards in front of the exchange zone. The receiver may start running at this mark, but can only receive the baton inside the 22-yard passing zone.

- An infringement of a rule by one runner disqualifies the entire relay team.

- The DGWS recommends the following relay races: 220-yard shuttle relay (55 yards each), 300-yard relay (75 yards each), 440-yard relay (110 yards each), 880-yard relay (220 yards each), 880-yard medley relay (220, 110, 110, 440), plus shuttle hurdle relays. In AAU and international meets, the 440-yard relay and 880-yard medley relay are run in addition to the mile relay (4 x 440).

STRATEGY

For fundamental strategy related to preparing for a meet, see Chapter 13.

Relay racing strategy lies in properly placing the runners. This involves a knowledge of the distances each person is to run, each person's ability to run these distances, and the ability of the opponents.

When all four girls are of equal ability, the best starter and the best combinations of girls who work well together should be considered.

If there is one slow girl, she should run the least distance with the baton, receive it near the end of her passing zone, and pass it near the beginning of the next zone.

For the medley relay (220, 110, 110, 440), set up the marks for passing and receiving so that the 220-girl passes the baton in the beginning of her zone and the 440-girl receives it near the end of her zone. Each girl will then have a shorter distance to cover.

6

Hurdling

DESCRIPTION

Low hurdles are 2 feet 6 inches (30 inches) and high hurdles are 2 feet 9 inches (33 inches) in height. Techniques for both skills are described as a unit with specific references where they are applicable. A former world record holder from Australia, Pam Kilborn, has listed several adjustments that she had made in switching from low to high hurdles, which are incorporated in the description below.

The hurdler must try to sprint over the hurdles with minimum interruption of normal sprint action. Hurdling is essentially a form event, and form can be learned. The process may be long and tedious, but there have been many "made" champions who have reached the top by courage, tenacity of will, and patience.

The first consideration in hurdling is to determine the lead leg—the first leg to go over the hurdle. The lead leg is generally the kicking leg in jumping and the back leg in the starting block. If the prospective hurdler has not tried a jumping event, the following learning experience will be of help.

Drill for Selecting the Lead Leg
Place a hurdle a few strides in front of you, and have a partner stand on the side of it. Go over the hurdle, one leg at a time. The observer should note which leg crossed the hurdle first. Repeat several times, checking if the same leg is used each time.

Drill for Lead Leg Lift, Push, and Snap
The lead leg should execute an elongated stride at the hurdle. It is

Fig. 6.1. Hurdling Takeoff and Landing. Lead leg shift (a), lead leg snap down (b)

brought up fast, knee first, and the heel aims at the top of the hurdle to be cleared. When the lead leg is 12 inches clear of the hurdle, it should snap down so that initial contact with the ground is on the toes of the lead leg. This snapping down will cause a slight dip in the body, which will assist in lifting the trail leg through. The trail leg bends so that the inside of the thigh passes over the hurdle.

Stand 2 to 3 feet in front of the hurdle. Step over the hurdle by raising the lead leg (knee first) and pushing with the trail leg. Snap the lead leg down and bring the trail leg through. Repeat this lift, push, and snap several times, and jog between each takeoff.

Arms should be used to prevent twisting of the body. The lead arm (opposite lead leg) should aim toward the top third of the hurdle ahead while the lead leg is being lifted. The other arm flexes at the side. As the lead leg hits the ground, exaggerate the arm action to avoid the natural tendency of the trunk to twist toward the trailing leg as it clears the hurdle. The sweep back of the leading arm must be *emphasized but controlled,* and the opposite arm must assist it by punching vigorously forward and slightly across the chest. The two arms work together in a somewhat circular action, which helps to keep the trunk facing forward.

The hurdler's center of gravity should not be raised to clear the hurdle. This will depend on the height of the hurdle. If the runner is able to straddle a hurdle flat-footed without her crotch touching the hurdle, she should raise neither head nor hips to clear it. This is not always possible in the women's high hurdle. The force necessary to ensure maximum speed can be attained only when one foot is in contact with the ground. While jumping over the hurdle, sprint action is minimized the longer the hurdler stays in the air. In order for the hurdler of average height to keep close to the ground, the trunk must lean forward slightly when the takeoff leg leaves the ground. (The taller hurdler needs less lean.) The landing on the other side of the hurdle should be no more than one and a half feet from the hurdle. This can be achieved by the cutdown of the lead leg. However, this cutdown should not place the leg behind the body's center of gravity; this would cause the same loss of momentum as if the leg were too far ahead.

Drill for Lead Leg Action
Place an object about 2 inches high on top of the hurdle, just off-center, toward the side of the lead leg. Jog toward the hurdle. While crossing it, knock off the object with the foot of the lead leg. Repeat several times, increasing speed as confidence builds.

Make every effort to follow through with the trailing leg, which is bent at the knee and parallel to the ground. Toes should point upward toward the knee. This ensures knee, ankle, and foot clearance. The importance of the action of the trail leg is second to that of forward body lean only. An extremely fast yet relaxed pull-through of the trail leg cannot help but speed up the downward snap of the lead leg.

As the rear foot loses contact with the ground, the leg must trail until the front foot is in position to drive down. When the body is on top of the hurdle, the back knee should be well in back of the top of the hurdle. If the back leg is brought through too soon, the advantage of the scissors action will be lost. (This improper action is closer to jumping.) The legs must act against each other, or they will be unbalanced and the action will be unnatural.

Drill for Strengthening the Trail Leg
Set up four hurdles, each one step apart. Step forward on the lead

Trail
leg

Lead
leg

Trail
leg

Trail leg after
full swing–through,
enabling a full complete
stride

Fig. 6.2. Hurdling Trail Leg Clearance. Trail leg clearance (a), trail leg after full swingthrough, enabling a full complete stride (b).

leg so that it is about 12 inches in front of the first hurdle. Bring the trail leg up and across the hurdle. Repeat stepping over the four hurdles without stopping. Remember to keep the torso straight and to bring the trail leg to hip level *because* the purpose of this exercise is to strengthen the trail leg's lifting muscles.

The motion should be continuous once the trail leg leaves the ground to clear the hurdle. The leg should clear and immediately reach out for the next stride. This involves pulling the lower leg through from the knee as soon as the foot clears the hurdle. There is very little thigh movement in low hurdling. (See arrow denoting path of the lower leg in Fig. 6.2.) Such an action is quite different from the usual high hurdle technique. High hurdlers must bring the thigh well forward before straightening the leg. This results in an additional movement that should be eliminated in low hurdling. The trail leg

must not come through above the horizontal for low hurdles. Failure to maintain the forward lean as the second leg comes through is a common fault, and hurdlers who tend to "sit up" as they come off the hurdle usually find themselves hitting it with the trailing foot or ankle.

Drill for Lead and Trail Leg Action
Place four hurdles about 7 feet apart. Go over them, taking one full stride between hurdles. Do not drop the trail leg close to the lead leg. Listen for a two-count landing—one sound for each foot. If a single thud is heard, you are jumping and not running.

The trail leg is brought through, and the hurdler is now ready to sprint two more strides to clear the next hurdle. This makes *three* sprinting steps before reaching takeoff for the next hurdle. The first stride occurs when the trail leg touches the ground.

Drill Three Strides Between Hurdles
When training for low hurdles, set up four hurdles, 26 feet 3 inches apart. The distance from the starting line to the first hurdle is 39 feet 4½ inches. From a standing start take seven strides to the first hurdle and three strides between each.

Difficulty in reaching the next hurdle in three strides is attributed to one or more of the following:

1.   failure to bring the trail forward for a full stride
2.   loss of balance due to improper arm or body carriage
3.   inability to take a full stride
4.   fatigue

The first two points require a review of hurdling techniques and clearance. Correct sprint practice will increase speed and lengthen the stride.[3] If fatigue is the problem, repeated conditioning over the hurdle will build up endurance. If the race calls for eight hurdles,

Fig. 6.3.   Mamie Rallins, an Olympic participant and former American record holder, moves toward victory in the 100-meter high hurdles at a National AAU Championship Meet. Photo *b* shows perfect coordination and placement of the lead leg and opposite arm position. This photo also illustrates an important technique of running the 30-inch and 33-inch hurdles—that is, on the lead leg, the knee is first brought up to clear the hurdle, there is not a swing of the full leg as for men in high hurdling form. Note snap-down of the lead leg close to the hurdle (World-Wide Photographers).

work several times over ten hurdles during practice sessions devoted to conditioning. If ten hurdles are the total for a race, work several times over twelve hurdles during the conditioning sessions.

A hurdler should sprint from the starting blocks to the first hurdle, between hurdles and off the last hurdle to the tape or finish line.

The first hurdle should be reached in seven steps. If it is difficult to reach the first hurdle with a sprint action or correct leading leg, do not attempt to deliberately lengthen the stride. Instead, practice starting with the opposite leg forward, thereby using eight steps. Then, sprint between the hurdles and past the tape.

Drill for Starts over First and Second Hurdles
From the starting blocks, practice going over the first hurdle six times. Expand the practice, and go over the first two hurdles. If the wooden hurdle is somewhat frightening, a piece of string may be stretched across the track instead. Do not allow the string to become a crutch, however.

MECHANICAL PRINCIPLES OPERATIVE AT CRITICAL PARTS OF HURDLING

Loss of velocity due to change in direction of velocity at each hurdle can be avoided by developing a run, rather than a series of jumps, to keep the center of gravity low.

Newton's third law states: For every action there is an equal and opposite reaction. Force for reaction is provided by pushing against the ground and extending with the takeoff leg and foot.

Applying the principle of opposition and transfer of momentum, the opposite leg (lead leg) and arm are brought forward.

Movement of a segment downward creates downward movement of force, which brings the leg down and keeps the center of gravity low. The body bends forward in a dip, thereby keeping the foot under the center of gravity.

Reaction to angular movement is balanced by rotation in the opposite direction. In the hurdles the opposite arm of the lead leg is brought forward to maintain balance.

If head and feet move down when the body is free in the air, the hips move up and vice versa. The hurdler chops the lead leg and brings it sharply down, with her toes pointing toward knees and parallel with the ground.

A body loses equilibrium when it falls outside of its base. The moving of the center of gravity outside the base is a prime requisite

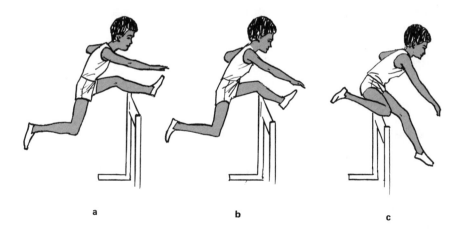

a   b   c

Fig. 6.4. Pam Kilborn, Australian high hurdle champion and former world record holder. Note how she skims the hurdle, as opposed to being too high over it. Her knee is lower than her heel. The author advocates this technique in running the 30-inch, or low, hurdles; however, in the 33-inch, or high hurdles, this could be a costly error for a person of shorter stature.

to continuing motions. The hurdler lands behind the center of gravity, thereby ensuring the momentum for the next hurdle, and so on, to finish the race. The next step after clearing the hurdle must be a definite stride, but not an overstride that might check momentum by shifting the center of gravity too far behind the front foot of support.

COMMON ERRORS AND CORRECTIONS

Balking at the Hurdle

This is frequently caused by fear of the hurdle. Use a string or breakaway hurdle for practice until the girl can go over the string with confidence.

Irregular Run to First Hurdle

Practice starting and going over the hurdle. Check takeoff point and adjust blocks or first steps out of blocks accordingly.

Too High over Hurdles

This is indicated by not enough forward lean or taking off too close to the hurdle. Check the lead leg landing over the previous hurdle. If the landing is too faraway, the next hurdle will be taken too closely.

Off-Balance over Hurdles

Work on these techniques: arm position for counterbalance and dip over hurdle.

Too Many Steps Between Hurdles

If the stride is not long enough, review the techniques of foreleg reach to obtain an additional 6 to 8 inches.

Kicking Hurdle with Lead Leg

If the takeoff line is too close, move it back. See that dip over hurdle is not exaggerated. Avoid straightening up when on top of the hurdle.

Kicking Hurdle with Trail Leg

Keep thigh and knee parallel to hurdle. Point toes back toward knee. Is the body too erect while passing over hurdle? Work on flexibility exercises (Appendix H) to loosen the hip area for unrestrained movement of the trail leg.

Losing Speed at Finish

Emphasize over-distance running. At practice periodically use an additional two hurdles, spaced at official distances.

Landing with a Severe Jolt

Don't land on the heel. Keep weight forward to land on ball of foot.

TEACHING PROGRESSION

Teach or work on the following:

    stretching exercises applicable to hurdles

    selection of lead leg

    lead leg action
        walking over hurdle
        jogging over hurdle
        running over hurdle

trail leg action
  walking over side of hurdle
  jogging over side of hurdle

total action over hurdle (using string or breakaway hurdle if hurdler is afraid)

three steps between hurdles

seven steps to first hurdle (eight steps with feet reversed at starting position)

starting over first two hurdles

full flight of hurdles

RECOGNIZED DISTANCE FOR THE HURDLES

Height of Hurdle	Distance of Race	Number of Hurdles	Distance from Start to First Hurdle	Distance Between Hurdles	Distance from Last Hurdle to Finish Line
30 in.	50 yds.	4	39 ft. 4½ in.	26 ft. 3 in.	31 ft. 10 in.
33 in.	50 yds.	4	42 ft. 7¾ in.	27 ft. 10½ in.	23 ft. 8¾ in.
33 in.	60 yds.	5	42 ft. 7¾ in.	27 ft. 10½ in.	25 ft. 10¼ in.
30 in.	70 yds.	6	39 ft. 4½ in.	26 ft. 3 in.	39 ft. 4½ in.
30 in.	80 yds.	7	42 ft. 7¾ in.	27 ft. 10½ in.	30 ft. 1¼ in.
33 in.	100 meters	10	42 ft. 7¾ in.	27 ft. 10½ in.	34 ft. 5½ in.
30 in.	200 meters	10	52 ft. 6 in.	62 ft. 4 in.	42 ft. 7¾ in.

RULES

- High hurdles for women are 33 inches. These include ten hurdles over a distance of 100 meters.
- Low hurdles are 30 inches.
- A hurdler is disqualified if her entire body does not go over the hurdle. She is not penalized for knocking down a hurdle.
- Hurdle relays consist of four persons to a team running in a shuttle formation.

STRATEGY

For fundamental strategy related to preparing for a meet, see Chapter 13. Strategy needed for hurdles does not differ from that for sprinting; therefore, that section in Chapter 2 (pages 26—27) should be reviewed.

National Competitors Participating in Two Field Events—Javelin (*a*), shot put (*b*) (World-Wide Photographers)

Part II

FIELD EVENTS

Two main divisions of field events are included in this section: jumping events (long jump and high jump) and weight, or throwing, events (shot put, discus, and javelin). These events are grouped into these categories because of their many common features: methods of teaching, application of scientific principles, terminology, training techniques, rules governing the event, and strategies related to the competitive situation.

The following basic principles are related to efficient performance in each field event:

- Maximum controlled momentum is built up in the approach.
- The action flows from this controlled momentum into the most effective power position from which to raise the body or thrust the implement.

- Follow-through results from the action that has taken place before rather than a separate consideration.
- Maximum performance is a result of a full-flowing total action rather than a segmented executed. The difference between these two lies primarily in the methods by which the principles are implemented.

Because of the overwhelming similarity of strategies related to the competitive situation, the following suggestions will be helpful for all field events. (For fundamental strategy related to preparing for a meet, see Chapter 13).

- Consider all conditions that might affect the approach steps—such as loose runways, slippery surfaces, and high winds. Then make the necessary adjustments.
- Understand the time lapse between trials; the athletes will keep their muscles warm by wearing sweats until they compete again.
- If the athletes are participating in more than one event, they should take as few trials as necessary.
- An excellent performance on the first trial puts a competitor far ahead of the others; therefore, she might consider passing the second and third trials.
- Remove sweats during competition, as they alter timing and cause unnecessary expenditure of energy.
- Try to avoid fouls on the first attempt. A relaxed effort not necessarily up to capacity often gets an athlete in the right frame of mind and removes undue pressure on the next attempt.
- In throwing events (javelin and discus), throw the implement *low* into a head wind and *high* into a tail wind.

7

Long Jump

DESCRIPTION

The long jump consists of four elements:

a fast run (approach)
a high jump (takeoff)
flight in air
landing

Each of these must be learned separately and completely.

Approach

The length of the run is determined by the shortest distance within which one can achieve optimum speed and still be prepared for the jump for height at the toeboard. Girls vary the length of their run from 80 to 115 feet.

Exercise to Establish Length of Run
The girl stands on the toeboard with her back to the pit. An observer is stationed about 90 feet from the pit. The run down the runway should be an attempt to build up optimum speed. The observer marks the point at which the runner reaches optimum speed. The observer moves this mark forward or backward depending on the consistency with which the board is missed.

This approach should be attempted ten to twelve times at each practice. Variables affecting the proper reaching of the toeboard

a	b	c	d

Fig. 7.1. **Long-Jump Float** (Sitdown-in-Air Style). Approach (a), takeoff (b), in air (c), landing (d)

(such as extreme wind, fatigue, a lengthened or shortened stride, and inconsistent strides) should be avoided. In the approach, strides must be consistent. Therefore, the long jumper must be aware of the stride lengths taken in each run.

Drill for Practicing the Approach
The jumper stands on the mark and faces the pit. She then runs forward, bearing in mind the proper form through the pit. She should not concentrate on the toeboard, but an observer should mark where the takeoff foot touches the ground. Practice this several times, always attempting to keep the strides consistent. If the jumper hits the same spot but does not touch the board, adjust the starting mark and move it the same distance as the spot is from the board. If she fails to hit the same spot, check for form—especially stride lengths.

The run should be relaxed. Speed is not the main concern since the runner must prepare her body for a forceful lift into the air when she reaches the toeboard.

Takeoff

In the last four strides of the run, shift attention to jumping—*not running at top speed*—and to jumping as high as possible.

Fig. 7.2.   Body Positions at Takeoff. Don't drop head and slump (a), do lift eyes and head, arch back, lift knee and arms during takeoff (b)

The takeoff foot (forward foot in starting block) hits the board almost flat-footed. The heel touches the ground slightly before the ball of the foot. Toes point directly forward, and the knee is slightly bent. At this point the center of gravity (point around which weight is evenly distributed) is directly over the foot. If the last stride is shortened, the center of gravity will be in front of the takeoff foot; if lengthened, the center of gravity will be behind. In either case, maximum jumping height will be curtailed. Extending the takeoff leg must be coordinated with raising and upwardly swinging the free leg, and a rocking motion up onto the toes of the takeoff foot. At this time, the head and chest should be driven upward and the back should be arched. The action of the kicking leg (back leg in the blocks) involves lifting the leg vigorously, knee first, toward the shoulders.

Exercise for Jumping for Height (pop-ups):
1.   Two girls hold a string, or a hurdle or bar 4 feet in front of the board at a height of 2 feet 6 inches to 3 feet 6 inches. The jumper takes four or five strides and takes off, concentrating on her form. In order to clear the obstacle and land in the pit, she must spring

Fig. 7.3.   Float or Sitdown-in-Air Style. This athlete is jumping 18 feet with this technique. Notice a common error typical of this style: The girl's chest and head are lowered to her knees rather than her knees brought up high toward an upright torso.

in the air. If the jump is successful, raise the obstacle. (Remind the runner about proper form; she should not attempt to use the obstacle as a crutch.) Then, remove the obstacle and have her attempt to reach the same height.

2. Follow the drill above, but use *two* obstacles the same height but 3 feet apart. This will teach the technique of keeping the legs up for a longer period of time.

Flight in Air

There are three styles of form in the air:

"float" (sitdown position in air)

"hitch-kick"

"hang"

It is impossible to increase body momentum after losing contact with the ground; therefore, "running in the air" and various forms of hitch-kicking are used mainly to give the athlete aerial balance or to aid in elevating her feet. *The most efficient and simple form for beginners is the knee-at-shoulders, or sitdown in the air, position—the "float" style.*

Fig. 7.4.   Hitch-kick. Using the left leg (a) to get the desired lift (b). Body twist at this phase of the lift will prevent reaching the desired height (World-Wide Photographers).

Fig. 7.5. Wyllie B. White illustrates the hang style. She jumps 21 feet 1 inch. Wyllie has been on four Olympic teams. Note her high knee action in her approach (*a, b*). She approaches not as a sprinter, but with more bouncy and springy steps, so that she gets maximum spring as she takes off from the board (World-Wide Photographers).

In the *float* style, the knees are brought up toward the shoulders with great force; the jumper holds this position as she "floats" into the landing. *Remember:* From takeoff the chest and head must be held high and the back must be erect. The lead leg thrusts toward the shoulders and the takeoff leg follows in the same motion. When both feet are raised to a sitting position (knees at shoulder height), the body balances to keep the buttocks from touching the pit. (See Fig. 7.1.)

In the *hitch-kick* style, the jumper takes a stride and a half in the air. It is advantageous in that the jumper may maintain her balance in the air. The movement in the air does not increase momentum. The hitch-kick emphasizes lead leg action; the lead leg is driven forcefully upward and forward. As the takeoff leg is brought forward (also with great force), the lead leg drops back. Then, as the takeoff foot reaches its greatest height, the lead foot is again driven forward to its best position for landing.

Fig. 7.6.   Hang style

In the *hang* style the athlete reaches maximum height with her chin and chest up, back slightly arched, and feet trailing behind the rest of her body. This form is greatly preferred because it further emphasizes the upward leap of the takeoff. After the board is cleared, the face points upward, the chin is lifted high, and the back arches. Quite naturally, the legs and feet drag well behind. Arms maintain balance. They are usually forward and out during flight. For an instant, the jumper seems to hang in the air. As she reaches the crest of her flight, there must be a forward swing of her hips to make it less difficult to lift her feet. As hips come forward, the legs are thrust ahead and the feet are brought up so that heels are about hip level. With arms also forward there is now a slight forward curve of the back. In this sitting position, feet are about a foot apart and knees are slightly bent. When properly executed, this is a sound style that is used more frequently than any other by long jump champions.

Landing

In landing, the jumper must continue in the forward direction. As she starts dropping toward the pit, she relies on strong abdominal muscles to keep her feet from touching too soon. The most practical method of landing is to extend the legs and spread the feet about a foot apart so that the body may go between the knees and over the feet when the pit is touched. The body must fall or pass beyond the

a   b   c

Fig. 7.7. Common Error in Executing the Hang Style. An athlete attempts the hang style for the first time, and demonstrates a common error in the hang style action. The jumper is arching (head starting back before she reaches maximum height) too soon (a). Also, she does not have sufficient height (b) to extend her legs fully before landing.

point where the heel strikes the pit. Four techniques are used to get past and over the feet:

1. the athlete drops her chin on her chest
2. leans forward from her hips
3. flexes her knees
4. swings her arms downward and backward

These techniques, taken in sequence, will prevent her from falling back into a sitting position.

Exercise for Landing
Take four or five strides, take off, and float. Concentrate on proper landing techniques. Select the best technique to get the body past the feet. Unless a jumper is able to obtain maximum height at take-off, she will not have time to obtain balance in the air and execute the necessary movements for proper landing.

All elements described—approach, takeoff, position in the air, and landing—are really a sequence of actions rhythmically synchronized and built into one action. At no time—from starting point to landing—can the athlete stop or hesitate. The total jump should now be practiced, with emphasis on proper form. Check periodically to correct faults or to denote areas that require concentration in part practice.

MECHANICAL PRINCIPLES OPERATIVE AT CRITICAL PARTS OF THE LONG JUMP

Principle of continuity: A body continues in its state of rest or of uniform motion in a straight line except insofar as it is compelled by forces to change that state. Make the approach with a uniform measured stride involving progressive acceleration. It should be sufficiently long enough to obtain the desired velocity. Bouncy steps may be more helpful than an all-out effort to build maximum velocity.

Principle of opposition: In the approach, the left arm is forward while the right leg is forward.

In order to gain maximum distance in jumping there must be a careful integration between the development of velocity (speed of movement) and height of projection. In the last three or four strides from the board, the jumper crouches in order to get her takeoff leg out in front of the center of gravity. She must take off with as much forward velocity and with as much upward thrust as possible for the longest jump. *Force times velocity equals force as the body is frequently put in motion by the transfer of momentum from a part to the whole.* To assist in upward thrust or lift, the arm should swing upward and the lead leg should swing up as high as possible.

A muscle will lose its elasticity if put under stretch too often and for too long a period of time. The approach should be of such length as to eliminate fatigue as a factor in obtaining the desired velocity.

Angular velocity is inversely proportional to the length of the radius. As the takeoff foot leaves the board, the leg should bend at the knee in order to bring it forward faster.

The direction of a body free in the air is determined by the direction of forces which set it in motion. The height to which the center of gravity can be raised above the floor cannot be affected by body movements, but the position of the center of gravity within the body can be changed and the body may be lowered or raised above the ground by movement or change in the position of a member of the body. No follow-through tactics or movements of members of the body while in air can change the direction or height of the body's center of gravity. The flight through air such as running does not enable the body to exert greater horizontal forces or velocity. It can aid in balance and will not be a detriment unless the legs are carried in such a manner as to impede forward progress.

Reaction of a short lever is not as great as the reaction of a long lever. When performing the hitch-kick, the leg is thrown back in a long lever (long radius) so that reaction to the hip region is forward with the head going backward. Head and shoulders lift up, and the back arches. Legs raise and come together, and head and shoulders are brought forward by bending at waist into an "L" position.

Newton's third law: For every action there is an equal reaction. Just before landing, arms swing backward.

The longer the lever the greater the distance. Bring feet as far out in front as possible. The center of gravity should be high relative to the point of support so that the forward component of force will be greater than the downward component. When feet hit the pit, knees bend to prevent falling backward, thus enabling the center of gravity to slide down the line of flight forward. The center of gravity lands at a lower level than at the instant of takeoff.

COMMON ERRORS AND CORRECTIONS

Legs Hit Pit While the Rest of the Body Falls Forward

The jumper raises her legs high, in the air. The initial jump was not strong enough.

Falling Back in Pit on Landing

If this happens, the arm action probably was not vigorous enough. A more vigorous arm swing at takeoff and landing is called for. As feet strike the sand, arms should swing sideward and forward. Knees bend at landing and head drops forward. Another fault could be overemphasized extension of the legs; however, it is rarely this, since most jumpers fail to carry their feet far enough ahead.

Low Jump

The athlete should jump harder and more vertically at takeoff; she should practice with string at hurdle height. Her head and eyes should be directed not toward the landing area, but forward and upward. Failure to straighten the leg and thigh deprives the jumper of some of the available force. Failure to utilize the potential in the free leg swing (caused by an incomplete rocking up on the toes) detracts from achieving maximum height. The center of gravity should be ahead of the takeoff foot at the moment the jumper leaves the board. Work at eliminating the erectness.

Landing at Side of Pit

Landing on the right or left side of the pit, or with one shoulder twisted forward, is caused by either running down the side of the runway or using a weak motion with one arm at takeoff.

Hitting Takeoff Board in Different Spot Each Jump

Frequently, the takeoff place differs with each jump—not necessarily on the board. This is caused primarily by a lack of uniform steps on the runway approach. Work on the approach. Schedule more 100- and 200-yard runs and work on consistency of stride.

Slow Run on Runway

The jumper lengthens her run to allow more time in building up speed.

Slowing Down at Takeoff

The athlete should practice pop-ups (takeoffs) for form. Use string for height. To avoid over-running, shorten run one-third of approach.

Tenseness and Lack of Speed

Concentrate on encouraging relaxation, just as the sprinters must do. Emphasize learning steps in the approach so that fouling is not uppermost in the jumper's mind.

Difficulty with Flight in Air

Before movements can be performed in the air, a sufficient amount of time in air must be provided. This can be accomplished only if height has been achieved at the takeoff. If the arch and leg extension are used, the arch must be formed at the height of the jump, not at the takeoff board. A common error is to start movements such as the hitch-kick in air or arch too soon—that is, immediately after leaving the board. There is also a tendency to continue these movements too long in the flight. This is caused if the jumper executes her movements too slowly or if she attempts to add an additional step, thereby preventing a proper preparation for landing.

TEACHING PROGRESSION

Teach or work on the following:

> selecting take off leg
>
> selecting starting point of the approach
>
> approach (running through steps)
>
> takeoff and vertical spring
>
> flight in air
>
> landing

RULES

- An official foul and trial is counted if any part of a jumper's body touches over the toeboard.
- The distance is measured from the mark closest to the toeboard.
- A foul is not measured and counts as a trial.
- Three trials are granted in both preliminaries and finals.
- One competitor more than the number of places is selected to compete in the finals. For example, seven contestants would enter the finals if six places—awards or points—were to be given.

STRATEGY

For fundamental strategy related to preparing for a meet, see Chapter 13. Strategy needed for long jumping does not differ markedly from other field events; therefore, these similarities in strategy are included in the Introduction to Part II.

8

High Jump

DESCRIPTION

The running high jump includes a run, a vertical jump, a layout over the bar, and landing. The style of the high jump is denoted by the position at the layout over the bar. There are four common styles:

scissors

"Eastern"

"Western roll"

straddle

The scissors is a style that is frequently the result of self-teaching. It is performed primarily in the lower grades. The scissors is the easiest yet least effective of the four methods.

The Eastern style is a complex derivation of the scissors and has practically disappeared from the American scene; however, a few athletes in international competition use a modified Eastern style. The Eastern is not only difficult, but also less economical, for it requires the athlete to gain a higher center of gravity than in any of the three other styles. The scissors and Eastern do not have the potential of the Western roll and straddle and, therefore, do not merit further discussion in this text. In national meets, the Western roll is less frequently performed than the straddle style. It is basically easier than the straddle, but its effectiveness has been questioned in recent years. The straddle style is discussed later in this section. A new innovation in high jumping styles is the "backward style" flop.

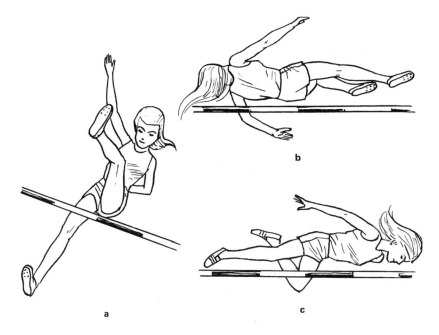

Fig. 8.1. **High Jumping Styles.** Scissors (a), western roll (b), straddle (c)

It is the technique identified with 1968 Olympic Champion Dick Fosbury. Although it is not described in this text, a sequence of photos of this style appears later in this section.

Approach

The run is not only as much a part of high jumping as the take-off or clearance, but is even more basic than these later phases. The run comes first and sets the pattern for the jump. If the run is weak or ill-timed, the jump will be equally so. The greater the height to be cleared, the more force (*speed times mass*) must be gained from the run. Perfecting the speed, rhythm, and coordination of the run is not merely helpful but also *essential* to great jumping.

The bar is approached from a 45-degree angle so that the kicking leg (back leg in the blocks) is the outside leg. The right-footed kicker runs from the left side. The simplest run is the seven-step approach, with the first step taken by the takeoff foot. During the run emphasis should be directed toward acceleration and relaxation—not speed. The first four steps are slow, whereas the last three must be smooth, quick, and progressively longer so that the takeoff foot is well ahead of the body weight. The only marks needed are the starting point and the takeoff point, which is about arm's length from the bar.

Exercise for the Approach
The jumper stands at the center of the bar, feet together, at arm's length from the bar, and faces the direction of the approach. Place a tape or chalk mark at this *takeoff point* (Fig. 8.2). The jumper runs away from the bar seven steps. Mark this point as the *starting point.* Practice running toward the bar until strides are smooth and uniform (no hop or skip), and the takeoff point is consistently hit.

Takeoff

The takeoff is concerned almost exclusively with jumping high. Jump high first and then think of clearing the bar. The takeoff combines horizontal momentum with vertical leap and includes the last few strides of the run. Since it establishes the direction and upward drive, the less it has to do with the method of clearing the bar the better. The concept of jumping high requires special practice. When done with a crossbar, it becomes confused with efficient clearance, proper form, and subconscious inhibitions. To explode upward with no concern for layout or landing is a technique that few jumpers have mastered.

Exercise for the Vertical Leap
Think of leaping up on a high platform, of the gather and crouch during the last few strides; of the backward lean of the body as it tries to break forward momentum; of the uplifted chest, chin, and eyes. Then, think of the explosive force that would bring the kicking leg to 6:05 o'clock. Finally, think how the arms would aid you—lowering with the crouch, driving upward with the body extensions.

Practice the takeoff as conceptualized above. Use three steps. It is unnecessary to practice by the pit; a grassy area may be used instead. This should be the manner of takeoff in the high jump, with no thought about anything except the jump for height. If this basic point of view is understood and practiced, the details of the technique will be mastered without special coaching.

Exercise for Takeoff
Set up the high jump standards without the bar. Use four steps several times, then go to seven. Concentrate on the lift. A partner should observe lean, heel plant, lift, balance, and kick.

Fig. 8.2.   High Jump Takeoff, Heel-Toe Placement Leap. Measuring takeoff (*a*), heel-toe placement (*b*), leap (*c*)

Western Roll (Layout)

Western roll clearance is a "layout" position on the top of the bar, with the side of the body nearly parallel to the ground (Fig. 8.3). As the kicking leg (right) is forcefully lifted, the takeoff leg (left) snaps underneath the right. Almost instantly the body turns toward the bar. Going over, the body's position is nearly parallel with the ground, with the head slightly raised. As the right leg kicks up, the left arm also extends and follows the right leg by a few inches across the bar.

In the layout position the lead leg (right) is relatively straight, and the takeoff leg is in a tucked position between the body and bar. The tucked knee is approximately at a 45-degree angle, and the entire leg is drawn as close as possible to the kicking leg. Bar clearance and the turndown toward the pit start with a slight back-kick

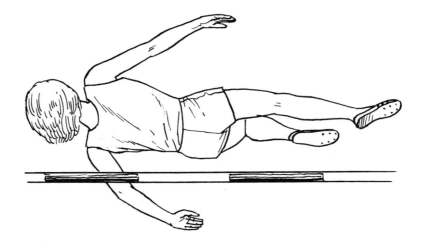

Fig. 8.3.   High Jump Layout Western Roll

with the lead leg (right), and the left arm drops toward the pit. Simultaneously dropping the head down and back aids in raising the hips for better clearance. The force necessary to carry the body across the bar is the forward momentum built up by the approach.

The roll or turn continues until the jumper is facing the ground. In the Western roll the actual landing takes place on the takeoff foot (left) and both hands. (*Note:* The pit surface must be soft enough to make the landing pleasant and to decrease or eliminate the fear of landing.)

Exercise for Western Roll Layout and Roll
Set the bar at about waist height or 6 to 8 inches lower than maximum height. Take three steps for the approach, takeoff, layout, and roll. A partner should observe the layout and roll positions, and make suggestions for improvement. Do this five or six times and add the regular seven-step approach. On landing, continue and concentrate on this position.

Straddle Style (Layout)

In the high jump, straddle style, the athlete straddles the bar on her stomach with her chest down. When taking off for the straddle clearance, the jumper should make certain that her outside arm does not come across her body. As in the Western roll, the kick should be along the bar and not over the center. These hints will

Fig. 8.4.   Western Roll Landing

prevent leaning into the bar at the takeoff. Again, not unlike the
Western roll, a high pendulum kick turns the body toward the bar,
but the takeoff leg does not tuck under. The secret in this style is to
master the hip roll for the takeoff leg lift. *Note:* The takeoff leg
(trailing leg) is most likely to hit the bar in this method of clearance.

At the top of the jump, *head action* plays a great part in lifting
the trailing leg. Just before reaching the point of maximum height,
turn the head back and slightly down, attempting to look at a spot
close to the point of takeoff. At the instant the head starts to turn,
straightening the trailing leg and simultaneously turning the toes on
the left foot toward the sky assist the trailing leg in clearing the bar.
During the clearance, the left hand is at the side. It must never get
between the body and the bar. The landing is made on the kicking
foot (right) and the outside hand (right). The athlete should let her
momentum roll her over on her side into the pit.

Exercise for Straddle Layout Technique

Take three approach steps toward the bar, kick up, straddle, and roll.
Practice five or six times with the bar at waist height, then use the
regular approach. A partner should check parts of the straddle form.

Fig. 8.5. High Jump Straddle

MECHANICAL PRINCIPLES OPERATIVE AT CRITICAL PARTS OF THE HIGH JUMP

Law of inertia and Newton's third law: For every action there is always an equal and opposite reaction. The run builds up momentum; speed is of little importance. The ability to spring is primary. Explosive power in springing is vital in attaining maximum height in the jump. The jumper, therefore, approaches the bar in comparatively slow loping movements until she is three or four strides away from the takeoff mark. In these last strides, the movement is relatively fast, with a crouch and spring in the last stride—in an attempt to stamp the foot hard so that the drive up will be as forceful as possible. The amount of crouch will be directly proportional to the strength of leg and thigh muscles.

In preparation for transforming horizontal force into vertical force, the center of gravity is within the base of support. The last step of the approach is the longest step of all. Lengthening the final stride enables the jumper to get the center of gravity inside the base of support.

Fig. 8.6. Backward Flop Style. Performed by a national high jump champion, Sally Plihal. She is clearing 5 feet 8 inches (World-Wide Photographers).

A body can be put in motion by the transfer of momentum from a part to the whole. To assist in the upward vertical lift after the plant, the free leg swings forward and upward while the arms swing up vigorously. An upward movement of the arms at takeoff adds to the lift. Arm movements must occur as simultaneously as possible; otherwise, because of the pull of the force of gravity, the entire body will lose its velocity before breaking contact with the ground.

Angular velocity is indirectly proportional to the length of the radius. If the lead leg is kept straight and a forceful swing upward is executed, the jumper achieves lift from the toe of his takeoff foot. Many jumpers doubt that they can throw a bent lead leg faster and be just as forceful. High jumpers who use a flexed leg swing depend more on eccentric leg thrust for their layout and, to some extent, sacrifice their spring. A leg can move with greater angular velocity when it is flexed rather than straight; however, this angular velocity is due to the reduced moment of inertia about the hip joints. The shortened radius cannot keep the jumper over the takeoff leg as long nor does it provide as high a position of her center of gravity at the instant of takeoff.

Layout efficiency in the high jump can be assessed by the body mass above and below the bar at this instant. The more mass the jumper has above it and the higher its position, the poorer the layout. Conversely, the more mass below the bar at the high point of the jump, and the nearer it is to the ground, the better the layout—provided, of course, that all parts of the body eventually clear the crossbar.

The straddle roll embodies these principles of the layout better than the other rolls, but the "backward flop" is a newer and greater innovation based on these principles. (See Fig. 8.6.) The straddle form seems to be the best method—not only because of the records attained, but because of the little effort and transference of forward momentum into vertical lift with minimum neuromuscular complexity.

For any body rotation at one end of the horizontal axis, there must be an equal and opposite rotation at the other end. The right arm passes over the bar toward the pit. At this point, Brumel (one of the world's greatest high jumpers) lifts his right arm back and toward the sky to help his left hip clear the bar. Once a high jumper is in the air, the trail leg will go down if the opposite arm goes up. If the jumper rotates his arms and shoulders in one direction, hips and legs will automatically rotate in the opposite direction. The proper mechanical movement would be to raise the leading arm at the peak of the jump in an effort to rotate the upper part of the body toward the back of the pit—thus raising the trail leg over the bar.

COMMON ERRORS AND CORRECTIONS

Approach

If the run is too long, the approach calls for a needless expenditure of energy. A run that is too short precludes the acquisition of sufficient momentum for crossbar clearance. If excess speed is generated, not enough time is allowed for executing the gather, foot plant, rock up on the toes, and leg swing. Careful practice on the approach is equally as important as concentrating on bar clearance techniques. Jump from approximately a 45-degree angle. Mark off the takeoff and start, and set up work between these steps.

Improper Lead Leg Kick

The lead leg should rise higher than the bar and aim at the *standard*—not at the bar itself. The kick must be high, hard, and strong. Exercises with a weighted shoe may help the weak kicker. Stress a high, hard kick.

Takeoff

Not jumping hard enough with the rear or takeoff leg is a major fault. The push (involving the muscles of the calf of the leg) and forceful straightening of the knee supply the jump. At takeoff, concentrate on jumping up rather than going over the bar.

Laying Out Too Soon or Too Late

The jumper must achieve vertical height before she lays out. She should try to throw both arms up as she leaps. This will tend to keep her head and shoulders up longer. If she lays out too late, she should turn her head and look down at the pit as she springs up from the ground.

Jumping Too Far or Too Close to the Bar

Jumping too far may be corrected by giving attention to the lead leg. The runner should move closer to the bar to correct the problem of taking off too faraway. Her takeoff mark should fall about one arm's length out from the bar; it may vary some, but not much, and her steps should be a little closer.

Conversely, if she is knocking off the bar before she reaches her maximum height, her steps should move away from the bar. When moving steps, move all of them—not just the takeoff step.

Failure to Rapidly Snap Up the Takeoff Leg

If snapping up the takeoff leg occurs too late after vertical lift, the jumper is likely to hit the bar when she is going up. To avoid this, concentrate on rapidly snapping up the takeoff leg.

Bar Clearance

In the Western roll, the left hip presents more difficulty than any other part of the body. Raise a low left hip by snapping the hip backward and to the left.

In the straddle style, many jumpers fail to elevate and straighten their takeoff leg when above the crossbar. Displacement of the bar is usually caused by contact with the inside of the left leg. A common correction is to have the jumper rotate her head to the left (left side approach) and look back toward the sky while over the bar.

TEACHING PROGRESSION

Teach or work on the following:

takeoff leg selection

establishing checkmarks

approach

kickup

layout (Frequently, this is taught prior to takeoff leg selection and establishing checkmarks. At this time, selecting the style of clearance should have been done.)

landing

RULES

- The height of the crossbar at starting and at each successive elevation shall be determined by the judges in charge of the event.

- A competitor may begin jumping at the starting height or any subsequent height. She may pass a jump at any height, and it will not be counted as a trial; a height may be passed even though she has failed it.

- Three consecutive failures at any height disqualify the contestant.

- The high jump bar will never be lowered. If a contestant leaves the high jump competition and returns with the bar at a higher height, her absence is recorded as a pass and she must jump the new height or higher if she still wishes to jump.

- Knocking the bar off the supports or touching the ground beyond the plane of the uprights with any part of the body (without clearing the crossbar) counts as a failure.

9

Shot Put

DESCRIPTION

The object of putting the shot is to *push the sphere from the shoulder*—not to throw it. To add momentum to the thrust, the athlete travels across a 7-foot circle before releasing it.

Shot-putting is usually learned in the following sequence:

the grip

the put from a stand

putting with total movement across the circle

Grip

The grip depends upon the strength of the fingers. The shot should rest on the base of the fingers, as high as good control and strength will permit. Holding it too high stiffens the fingers, hands, and wrist; holding it too low deadens the crack of the whip. The shot should be held low on the neck, with the elbow high.

Standing Put

The standing put involves a nonsegmented movement beginning with a lift from the right leg (right-handed putter), a rotation of hips and shoulders, and a full extension after releasing the shot. The standing put should not only serve as a warm-up, but also as a practice of good form. The putter should stand in the middle of the circle with her back to the board. She then drops over the right

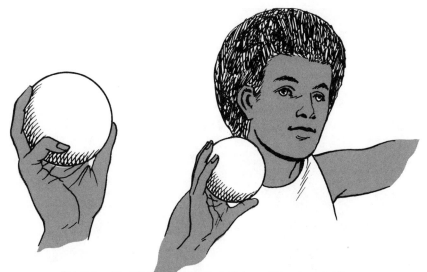

Fig. 9.1.   Shot Put Grip. Handhold (*a*), position at neck (*b*)

knee into a low crouch; shoulders are level with hips, and eyes are fixed on a point about 3 feet left of the center line behind the circle. The left arm comfortably flexes at shoulder height. The putter lifts from the right leg and rotates her hips and then the shoulders forward to release the shot while extending upward into the put. Once the shot leaves the hand, the right arm is pulled down across the front of the body and the feet are reversed. (The beginner should not reverse at this early stage because there is a tendency to release the shot with both feet off the ground, thus decreasing the amount of force which could be obtained.) Once the lift begins, the left arm is thrown back and down. Head and eyes should be raised toward the sky as the shot is released.

Exercise for Standing Put Movement
Stand in the circle, with back toward the board. Drop over the right knee into the crouch. Lift the left leg to be sure weight is on the right. Be sure that feet are at the 9:30 position. Shoulders and hips should rotate to the right. Now, push the right arm upward to release the shot. Do this in a sequential action several times, and ask a partner to observe whether or not arms moved correctly.

Holding the weight over the right leg can be difficult if the leg is weak. See Chapter 13 and Appendix E for the appropriate strengthening exercises.

Fig. 9.2. Shot Put Sequences. A most important facet of shot-putting—remaining in a closed, tucked position after the shift (c). This athlete could assume a greater closed position, thereby be able to generate more power in giving impetus to the shot. The shot-putter in (d) should have achieved greater extension (World-Wide Photographers).

In order to prevent a segmented action, lift and rotate the various body parts just before reaching the final position of each part. The action should then be smooth and rhythmical.

The "O'Brien" Method

Keep in mind the principles of wholeness of action and continuous acceleration of motion across the circle throughout the following discussion of the "O'Brien" form in the shot put.

For a clear understanding of the action across the circle, the entire action of the shot put will be described in the following parts:

stance in the rear of the circle
shift
impetus to the shot (release)
reverse

Stance in Rear

Action begins opposite the board. The putter places her foot on an imaginary line that passes through the center of the circle and the middle of the toeboard. The foot can be either perpendicular to a tangent and touching the back of the circle, or turned at a slight angle. The shot is comfortably situated on the neck and held in the right hand.

The Shift

With the body in balance, the putter now drops low over her right leg and drives; she maintains this low position to the center of the circle. During this drive, the weight of the hips is not over the right leg, but falls toward the toeboard, pulling the body off-balance. The heel is the last part of the right leg to leave the ground. Then, the leg is quickly pulled under the body. The right foot of the putter should now be in the center of the circle, the left leg almost straight at the board. Shoulders and head still face the back of the circle. The putter is low and in a "power position."

The Release

From here, the lift off the right leg begins. Then, hips and shoulders begin their rotation. The hips are driven up and around; the chest and head are also thrown up. This upward drive should be great enough to propel the thrower up on the toes of her feet. At the same time, the right arm pushes the shot upward and outward and it is released.

The Reverse

Once the shot has left the hand, the reverse is executed quickly. The reverse is a *result of the throw*—not part of it. The right arm is across the body; the right leg is at the toeboard and bent, while the left leg is high in back, also bent. If necessary, the putter may have to drive her body away from the board by placing her fingers on the inside of the board (not on top) and pushing.

The main objective of practicing is not to establish "how far," but *how.* It is best to work with two shots, with someone rolling them back to the circle. The puts should be taken with the idea of the whole action in mind, and all the following points should be checked:

1. position of the shot on the neck
2. achieve lowness in the back and center of circle
3. glide to the center—do not hop
4. correct position of the right leg is the center of the circle
5. lift of leg proceeds rotation of hips
6. hold chest and head high
7. the reverse is a result of the throw

MECHANICAL PRINCIPLES OPERATIVE AT CRITICAL PARTS OF THE SHOT PUT

Increase distance in which force can be applied, thereby causing force. Face rear of circle with right foot (right-handed putter) as close to the back of the ring as possible.

Law of continuous motion. Movement across the ring: Applied force on the shot must be continuous. Keep uniform acceleration. Starting and slowing down or stopping diminishes force developed.

Maximum force is exerted when all forces are in a straight line. The shot must travel in a straight line from start of movement across the circle to the point of release.

$P = FV$: *Power is equal to strength times speed.* Total body strength plus the ability to transform that strength into lightning-fast action is of great importance. By itself, strength will not give maximum horizontal distance. A smaller but faster individual may beat one who is slower and bigger.

Newton's third law: For every action there is always an equal and opposite reaction. No force can be exerted to move the body forward while the feet are not in contact with the ground. Therefore, feet must stay close to the ground in the glide.

With constant linear velocity, the angular velocity varies inversely with the length of the radius. The shot is held near the neck while in angular rotation.

Increase angular moment of force. The lead foot should be planted on the center line with the left foot slightly to the left. Therefore, there is a greater distance of area in which to apply force and more torque at the hips and shoulders. This also prevents angular motion from beginning too soon.

Mass in motion adds accelerating force. The center of gravity is started forward and upward before the body begins rotation.

A long lever enables a greater distance to apply force. The shot is moved in front of elbow. The left arm moves to the left, thus increasing the torque.

Newton's third law: For every action there is always an equal and opposite reaction. The putting foot must remain in contact with the ground during the entire thrust. For the right-handed putter, this is the right foot.

The movement of each member should start at the moment of greatest velocity but least acceleration of the preceding member. The forces to be added start with the right leg through the hips, back, shoulders, arm, and wrist action. The sequence of movements, then, should be such that just before one member completes its action on the shot, the action of the next should begin. When the arm goes forward past the shoulder, the arm is at its maximum velocity but least acceleration as the wrist snap is added. At wrist snap, slightly rotate the shot as it is released so that fingers push through the center of gravity in the direction of flight.

For equilibrium to exist, the center of gravity of a body must fall within its base. The reverse after the release is necessary to avoid fouling and to regain balance.

COMMON ERRORS AND CORRECTIONS

Improper Handhold

If the shot is too low in the hand, it prevents a full thrust of the wrist at the end of the put. Adjusting the shot higher on the fingers will correct this. Improper handhold is frequently only a symptom, however; the true cause may be lack of finger strength. Fingertip push-ups or other exercises will develop fingers or wrist strength.

If the shot is held too high on the fingers, it will slip backward of the fingers. Recheck handhold, paying particular attention to thumb and finger placement so that finger and thumb balance can be maintained. To avoid fatigue, carry the shot in the nonputting hand until ready to put.

Not Getting over Putting Leg

The putting leg should be under the shot after the shift. This enables maximum force to be exerted by that leg in a direction to the left of the body. The leg loses its effectiveness if it is not under the body. Practice the shift, concentrating on bringing the right foot more quickly under the body.

Stopping After the Shift

This common error is committed not only by beginners, but also by experienced putters. It is a serious flaw and must be eliminated. Sometimes it is caused by working too much on just the shift as a part of the action. To correct, the putter must execute the entire movement pattern as frequently as feasible.

Stopping after the shift might also be caused by landing flat-footed after the shift, which tends to cause the putter to settle in that position. The putter should remember to land on the ball of her right foot instead. If an athlete hops too high in the shift, she should keep her right foot close to the ground in a glide, rather than a hop.

Releasing Too Soon

If the shot falls too far to the right of the center line, the arm is coming through before full extension is begun from other sequential movements. The student should work on putting from a stand, emphasizing leg, hip, shoulder, and arms in a sequential pattern.

Releasing Too Late

If the arm is too slow in coming through, check to see if there has been an unnecessary movement—such as dropping the shot down to the shoulder before the forward thrust. For total sequential movement, work again with the put from a stand.

Putting on the Reverse or in the Air

These are serious and costly mistakes that must be eliminated early in practice. The putter may tend to allow the forward momentum gained during the shift and the push developed by the thrust of the rear leg to carry her into the air from where she completed the throw. The shot must be put from the ground; the body must have something against which to brace itself. This ground contact is important also because it delays the foot switch and keeps the center of gravity to the rear of the foul zone, thus helping to prevent needless fouls. The rear foot must be on the ground until the ball leaves the hand; the foot switch must be the result of forward momentum—not the cause of it.

TEACHING PROGRESSION

Teach or work on the following:

grip
putting from a standing position
starting position (in back of the circle)
glide
release
total movement
reverse
total movement and reverse

RULES

- The shot put weighs 8 pounds 13 ounces (4 kilograms) for college or open divisions, 8 pounds for high school girls, and 6 pounds for elementary school girls.
- The diameter of the shot-put circle is 7 feet.
- The shot must be put or pushed. A throw is counted as a foul.
- Three trials are given in both preliminaries and finals.
- Stepping on or over the toeboard is a foul.
- A foul counts as a trial but is not measured.

10

Discus

DESCRIPTION

The Grip

The hand is placed on the top of the discus, with fingers spread comfortably apart. The edge of the discus is in the first notches of the fingers as the discus rests against the palm. The farther the forefinger (right-handed thrower) is to the left of the center of the discus, the greater the rotating force that can be given, and the less chance of slipping out. However, the forefinger must hold its grasp and force the discus to rotate around it. Release the discus by closing the fingers; leave the forefinger last and rotate clockwise.

Exercise for Hand Action
To grow accustomed to the hand action and rotating the discus, let it roll off the fingers onto the ground. *Remember: Forefinger last, rotate clockwise.* Repeat until this action has been learned.

Throwing from a Stand

The thrower works for form and warms up by taking some standing throws from the circle. Days or weeks may be spent participating throwing from a stand until the "feel" of throwing the discus is attained.

The right-handed thrower faces the back of the circle, with feet even and shoulders level. She takes a step forward on her right leg while swinging the discus back easily. Eyes should be horizontal at

a   b

Fig. 10.1.   Discus Grip (*a*) and Release (*b*)

all times. Once over the right leg, the body is lifted off the leg, thereby driving the hips and chest upward while pulling through with the
right arm. The right arm is never dropped below or close to the hip,
but is held between the shoulders and hips away from the body as
the throw is started. The right arm continues upward, and the discus
is released at shoulder level. The stance should not be too wide, or
the hips might not be lifted properly. Feet should be about shoulder-
width apart. The reverse is a quick exchange of the feet, but results
from built-up momentum which is not great in the standing throw.
As in shot-putting, the release should not be attempted at this point
in acquiring technique.

Exercise for Throwing from a Stand
Draw a straight line through the center of a discus circle. Practice
the techniques of throwing from a stand. When stepping forward on
the right foot, place it on the center line (the left foot should be
slightly behind the line). Practice this several times. Then have a

Fig. 10.2.   Discus—Standing Throw

partner check shoulders, feet, eyes, weight distribution, position of the discus in the hand, and upward drive. A trajectory of more than 30 degrees is essential for greater distance.

Secure this trajectory by bringing the discus not more than 6 inches below shoulder height as it reaches the midpoint of the throw.

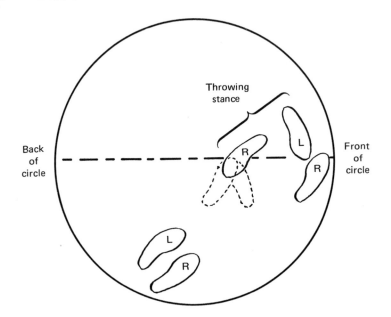

Fig. 10.3. Discus Step Forward and Pivot. Back of circle (*a*), throwing stance (*b*), front of circle (*c*)

The right arm is at right angles to the direction of the throw. A common error in attempting a higher trajectory is to tilt the discus on the release by bending the wrist backward toward the shoulder. *Remember:* To have a flat release, palms must face the ground.

Leading Up to the Turn

Learning to step forward and pivot as an extension of throwing from a stand is one motion closer to learning the rhythm of the turn. The thrower should face the direction of the throw with her feet even and the side of the left foot to the right of the center line. Hold the discus behind but away from the body. As the discus reaches an extreme backward position, take a step forward (about 12 inches) onto the ball of the right foot, while smoothly pivoting to a position identical to that taken when throwing from a stand. Make the throw from this position; the throw is made as previously described.

Exercise for the Step and Pivot
Follow the directions above. Remember to step on the ball of the right foot. Keep the right shoulder back until hips have rotated. Review the techniques of throwing from a stand. Walk through the first

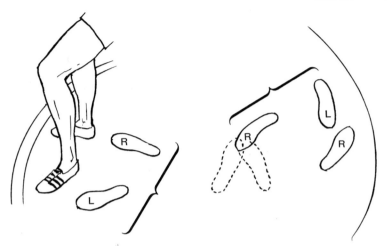

Fig. 10.4. Discus Foot Placement During Turn

attempts. Later, supplement the pivot on the right foot with a twisting hop into the throwing position.

The Turn

To build up momentum, start a one-and-three-quarter turn at the rear of the circle, and continue through the reverse. In the discus, the turn is probably the most difficult phase of any field event to learn. Because of the necessity for maintaining balance, speed, and force during the turn, it is imperative that the thrower be secure in executing a throw from a stand.

The spin begins in the rear of the circle. Straddle an imaginary line through the center of the circle, with feet no further apart than shoulder-width. Head and shoulders should be level, with the weight on the right foot and the discus back and away from the hips. As the turn begins, the discus remains back and the weight shifts to the ball of the left foot, with the knees bent considerably. Keep the left leg in contact with the ground as long as possible.

As the thrower lifts her right leg, it passes close to her left knee, which is still bent, but starts to rotate toward the center of the circle. With her head still level and arm still back, she drives off her left foot toward the center of the circle. At the same time, her body undergoes a 180-degree turn and her right foot falls into the center of the circle pointing toward the rear. After this 180-degree turn to the left, the body is now in the position practiced when throwing from a stand.

Now the right arm should be in a cocked position, ready to come through quickly in a smooth, inclined plane. Immediately lift off the right leg, which was bent under the body, and drive the left leg down to the ground as the hips lift upward and around pulling the arm through. Final impetus is given by the right leg as it gets into the throw and by the final wrist snap and finger force as the discus is released. If the spin is executed properly, the thrower will be forced into a quick and almost simultaneous reverse (a quick exchange of the feet).

Exercise for the Turn
1. Practice the entire movement, emphasizing continuity rather than speed. Tape the discus to the hand so that it is neither released nor dropped and so that "how far" will be forgotten. Repeat many times.
2. Remove the tape. The thrower should think to herself, "turn and throw." Say it while practicing. Keep eyes on the horizontal, hold the discus back, and then go into the "turn-n-n-n and throw."

MECHANICAL PRINCIPLES OPERATIVE AT CRITICAL PARTS OF THE DISCUS THROW

Increase the distance over which force can be applied. Rotate the body so that you face the opposite direction of intended flight. Stand as close as possible to the back of the circle.

Maximum force is available when both angular and linear forces are employed. The spin integrates linear and angular movements.

The longer the radius, the greater the velocity. Radius of rotation should be as long as possible. Hold the discus over the first joint of the finger if hand size permits. Keep the nonthrowing arm close to the body in angular motion. At release it should form a long radius, tending to create a greater moment of force.

Law of Continuous Motion. The movement across the circle must be continuous for maximum force.

Increase angular moment of force. The discus should trail the shoulders and hips; this ensures more torque at the shoulders plus added force at the right angle. Upon completing the spin the lead foot is in an open position to allow for greater angular movement of the hips and trunk. This gives greater angular velocity.

Fig. 10.5.   Entire Movements in the Discus Throw

Newton's third law: For every action there is always an equal and opposite reaction. The throwing foot (right foot for right-handed thrower) must be in contact with the ground when power is transmitted into the throw.

The movement of each member should start at the moment of greatest velocity but least acceleration of the preceding member. Not unlike the shot put, the forces to be added to the actual throw are in sequence starting with the straightening of the throwing leg to the hip, back, shoulders, arm, and fingers.

Maximum force is exerted when applied at right angles to the direction desired. Release the discus at right angles to direction desired at shoulder level.

Speed of release is the factor of greatest importance. A small increase in speed in discus-throwing gives a comparatively larger increase in distance.

For a given speed, the most important variable is the angle of projection. Throwing at distances of 150 feet or more should project at 35 to 40 degrees; throwers of lesser ability should increase the angle slightly, but never above 45 degrees.

The attitude angle of release should be between 25 and 35 degrees. The greater the speed of the discus upon release and the stronger the opposing wind, the smaller should be the attitude angle as the discus leaves the hand. Stronger headwinds reduce stability in flight and, therefore, shorten the distance.

For equilibrium to exist, the center of gravity of a body must fall within its base. Reverse after a throw to remain inside the ring.

COMMON ERRORS AND CORRECTIONS

Arm Leading Shoulder in Throw

The hand must be pulled rather than pushed by the shoulder and chest. Practice this pulling action.

Jumping Off Ground at End of Throw

Keep both feet on the ground. Much of the force behind the platter is supplied by the push from the legs against the ground.

Not Coiling Down

Bending should be done at knees, hips, and waist.

Hand Not Horizontal Throughout the Movement

This is important to learn at the beginning. Throughout the discus throw the discus must be horizontal; consequently, the hand of the thrower must be horizontal. The arm supplies the upward momentum of the object. The hand stabilizes the discus and presents it into the air in the position from which the most glide will result. An upturned discus will catch the wind and create air resistance, thus cutting down the distance it will travel, whereas a more horizontal discus will cut the air and travel smoothly. The discus is held comfortably with the fingers spread, but not stretched apart, and with the edge of the discus resting against the outer joints of the fingers. It is released from the index finger.

Arm Swinging Forward in a Horizontal Plane

The arm is the force that supplies the discus's upward flight. It comes from a position about belt high to one even with the shoulder on the release. The discus will fly in a continuation of the angle which the arm describes coming forward. *Remember:* The *arm,* not the hand, sends the discus up; the discus itself must be horizontal.

Stumbling to Right or Left of Circle as One Turns

This is a result of imbalance and can be caused by a number of things. Most often, correct foot placement will correct this fault. In spinning, make certain that the right foot is placed on the center line rather than too far to the left or right. Stumbling can also result when the thrower travels in a diagonal direction; this can be corrected by calling the thrower's attention to the center line.

Falling Out of Circle as Discus is Released

See if the steps taken in the turn were not too large for the thrower, thereby causing her to bound across the circle. She should also avoid leaning too far forward as the discus is released. The thrower should extend upward into the throw. Faulty placement of the left leg (bracing leg) may have occurred. The left leg acts as a brake and, if used correctly, prevents this fault. If the right and left feet are too close together, the left leg is prevented from acting as a brace.

TEACHING PROGRESSION

Teach or work on the following:

grip

release

throwing from a stand

step and pivot

one-and-three-quarter turn

total action (turn and release)

total action and reverse (turn, release, and reverse)

RULES

- The discus ring is 8 feet 2½ inches in diameter.
- The discus weighs 2 pounds 3¼ ounces. The accepted diameter of the discus is between 7 and 3/32 inches and 7 and 5/32 inches. A metal or hard rubber discus may be used if it complies with all specifications. The official discus contains a metal center, wooden body, and metal rim.
- Valid throws must land within a 60-degree sector marked on the ground.
- The circle must be left from the rear. If a competitor leaves the circle from the side after competing, it is a foul.
- Measurement is from the nearest mark made by the discus to the inside circumference of the restraining circle.
- A foul throw is not measured and is counted as a trial.
- Stepping on or over the foul line is counted as a foul.
- Three trials are given in both preliminaries and finals.

11

Javelin

DESCRIPTION

The javelin throw involves building up optimum momentum without sacrificing the most powerful body position from which maximum force and velocity can be applied to the delivery of the sphere.

There are three acceptable styles of throwing the javelin:

American hop

Finnish

Russian

The American hop is practically nonexistent among experienced throwers because it involves slowing down while preparing for the throw and thus sacrifices optimum momentum. The Russian style is most difficult to master, for it requires an arch of the back and whipping of these muscles for greater force in addition to the regular sequential movements. The Finnish style, when properly executed, is the most efficient and practical form; therefore, it will be used in this description. Here, the athlete carries the javelin over the shoulder for running ease and uses a front cross-step to turn the trunk to a powerful throwing position.

Grips

The two most acceptable grips are illustrated in Fig. II.I. In both grips the javelin is placed diagonally across the palm, from

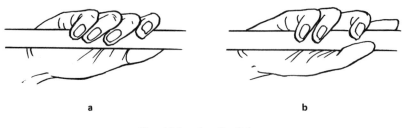

a   b

Fig. 11.1.   Javelin Grips

the base of the index finger to the heel of the hand. The grip in *b* is more desirable because the second finger can be strengthened beyond that of the first and the first finger can aid in slightly lifting the tail of the javelin. It is a comfortable grip that does not strain the arm.

Exercise for Grip and Carry
Try both grips and select the most comfortable. Is there a feeling of relaxation and flexibility while maintaining control of wrist, hand, and fingers? Take the javelin over the right shoulder. Walk with it, and grow accustomed to the carry.

Standing Throw

The most effective method of learning correct javelin delivery is from a standing position (Fig. 11.3).

The body's weight is over the bent right leg, and the left foot is planted firmly forward. The *left side* of the body faces the direction of the throw. The javelin is pulled back so that the right elbow is almost straight. The point of the javelin is about eye level. The body leans slightly backward from the hips, with head and eyes facing forward and upward. The momentum and force for the throw are begun by the upward and forward drive off the right leg, the forward and upward rotation of the hips, and the rotational pull of the left side of the body. Simultaneously, the throwing arm, now bent at the elbow, pulls the javelin forward. *The elbow is leading the hand* similar to the way a quarterback passes a football and not like a ball is thrown. The head rotates to the left, and the strong muscles of the trunk and shoulders have pulled the left side of the body to the left and back—not down.

Body weight is now up on the left leg as the javelin leaves the hand over the head. Wrist snap provides final impetus. The javelin leaves the hand at about a 45-degree angle to the ground in front of the right shoulder.

Fig. 11.2. Shoulder Carry

Exercise for Developing Delivery Technique
Learn to control flight of the javelin by throwing many times from a stand. Have a partner observe two or three parts each time you throw. Next walk a few steps into the throwing position before delivery.

Approach

Optimum momentum is provided by a running approach. The purpose of the approach is to initiate and accelerate the forward velocity of the javelin. Its length is determined by the distance in which the greatest speed can be attained and maintained in the cross-step. The approach must be rhythmical, smooth, and accurate before considering any thought of greater speed. A longer approach and more speed come with improvements in form and conditioning. Some coaches advocate three checkmarks, but the author recommends two:

Fig. 11.3.   Javelin Throwing Action

1.   the starting point
2.   the place where the cross-step is to begin

The first checkmark is from 11 to 13 running strides to the second. The second is about 25 to 35 feet from the foul line. This is illustrated in Fig. 11.4. It is important that stride length be determined accurately so that the left foot consistently hits the second checkmark, at the same speed.

Exercises for Determining Checkmarks and Approach
1.   *Checkmarks:* With the back to the foul line, run forward five strides. A partner marks this point, which is the second checkmark. Now, run forward about eleven strides. The partner now marks the first mark, or starting point. Measure these distances.
2.   *Approach:* Start on the left foot at the first mark. Allow the body to fall forward slowly as the run begins. Practice several times, carrying the javelin until strides are consistent. Then adjust the mark by one or two strides (preferably two), which again will enable a start on the left foot.

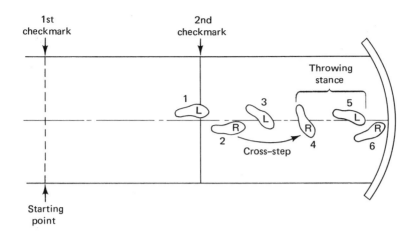

Fig. 11.4.   Checkmarks and Front Cross-Foot Placement

Cross-Step

From a run the athlete executes a front cross-step which allows her to turn her trunk to a powerful throwing position without sacrificing momentum.

A suggested count system for practicing the cross-step to get into the throwing position follows:

1. The left foot hits the second checkmark with toes facing forward; the javelin is starting to be pulled back.

2. The right foot lands in front of the checkmark with toes forward; the pull of the javelin to the back continues.

3. The left foot lands on the center line with toes pointing slightly to the right; the javelin is now well to the back.

4. The right foot crosses over in front of the left and lands parallel to the toeboard; the javelin starts forward, elbow leading.

5. The left foot goes into a long step and is planted just to the left of the center line with toes pointing forward in line with throw; the javelin continues forward.

After the fifth count the upper body is still going forward, but the left leg has checked the lower body and a whip action of the upper trunk is taking place. The javelin is pulled forward over and close to the head and is released in front of and about 12 inches above the head.

Exercise for Learning the Cross-Step

Draw a line down the center of the approach area from the starting point to the board.

Walk through the front cross-step into a throwing stance. Do not use the javelin. Use the rhythmic count of five:

1. feet at checkmark
2. step right
3. step left
4. cross right
5. step left

Repeat until the foot pattern is learned.

Hold the javelin and walk with it. Concentrate on body and javelin position on each count. A partner should observe each position.

The foregoing experiences should be repeated until the thrower is confident enough to increase her speed. Then the cross-step can be executed after including the approach. The thrower must remember the explosive and powerful body position discussed in the section related to throwing from a stand; it must be assumed with no hesitation after the left foot is planted following the cross-step.

Follow-Through

The follow-through or reverse results from the force built up from starting point until delivery. To check forward momentum (preventing a foul by touching or crossing the toeboard), the weight goes over into the right leg, which has come forward after the javelin has left the hand.

Finally, speed is an important factor in throwing the javelin. The effective transfer of running speed into useful throwing force is essential and requires much practice to perfect the transfer.

MECHANICAL PRINCIPLES OPERATIVE AT CRITICAL PARTS OF THE JAVELIN THROW

Principle of Opposition. In the approach, the left arm is forward while the right leg is forward.

A body continues in its state of rest or of uniform motion in a straight line except insofar as it is compelled by forces to change that state (Principle of Continuity: Newton's first law). The approach is with a uniform measured stride involving progressive acceleration. The javelin is in continuous motion.

Increase distance in which force can be applied thereby causing greater force. The approach should be of sufficient length so as to obtain the desired velocity (power equals force times velocity).

The muscle will lose its elasticity if put under stress too often and for too long a period of time. The approach should be of such a length as to discourage fatigue before obtaining maximum velocity.

Summation principle: If successively added, forces are to be added at maximum velocity and least acceleration of preceding phase. The total effective force is the sum of the forces of each member of the body.

Forward linear motion must be integrated with angular motion to obtain maximum velocity. The entire run, turn, and throw must be integrated.

Application of force must be continuous. The cross-step permits foot plant without losing linear motion.

Greater application of torque permits the body to rotate through a greater arc. Plant the foot in an open stance. As the lead (planted) foot is placed, the body tilts back with the center of gravity behind the foot. This permits the body to be placed in a more favorable position to exert force.

Distance added to force gives greater velocity. If the athlete is crouching and her throwing arm is back in a long drawn position, the abdominal muscles will pull the chest and arm around in the javelin throw, thereby developing torque. Simultaneously, the push-off leg, which is bent, is then extended.

Length of radius is directly proportional to linear velocity. Additional distance for a thrown implement is obtained by bending a joint and extending it just prior to release. Therefore, the elbow leads the hand in the javelin throw.

Optimum angle of projection is 45 degrees: There is a wrist snap at the very end of the movement. However, the javelin is released at an angle slightly less than 45 degrees.

A center of gravity which is lowered and inside the base of support will yield equilibrium. The reverse is executed.

COMMON ERRORS AND CORRECTIONS

A Too-Fast Approach

If the approach is too fast, enough time cannot be devoted to developing a powerful body position in order to get the force needed in the throw. Experiment until finding the best speed—that is, one that doesn't hinder or sacrifice a movement into a powerful body position.

Arm Coming Through Too Soon

The throw begins when the arm extends and is then brought forward. Among other things, moving the arm forward from an extended position allows the thrower time to gain force from her legs, hips, and shoulders. An error in this motion can be recognized if the javelin comes head high, or higher, before the body is square to the front. Work on the drills related to total body action before releasing the javelin.

Incorrect Body Turn in Cross-Step

The right toe tends to indicate how much turn will be in the hips. Teach turning the right toe out on the cross-step; this rotates the hips into a tucked position.

Throwing Stance Too Narrow

If too wide or too narrow, the throwing stance will alter the throwing distance because it will limit the power position that is essential in maximum performance. The position ought to be one that can generate a comfortable transfer of weight.

Throwing Side-Arm

This error puts undue stress on the throwing arm; distance is lost with a side-arm throw. Insistence on and practice of an over-the-shoulder and fairly straight-arm throw will correct this error.

Falling to the Left

The left side of the body and leg is used as a bracing force, and all movements must be carried and extended over that side of the body. If the left side is not firm, the needed extension is not possible. The athlete should work on the plant-and-drive-up-to-left-side without reversing. Falling away from the javelin also causes a side-arm throw rather than straight-through.

Strain and Effort vs. Relaxation

Those muscles that are not working must be relaxed. Tension is frequently created by an all-out effort all of the time. Throws should be made at nine-tenths or seven-eighths maximum effort. Discourage attempts to throw always beyond actual capacity. Work on form; distance will come.

Lack of Follow-Through

The follow-through is a result of what has gone before. If one has not generated force or power before the release, the release will not culminate in good follow-through. To correct, get at the cause, not the symptom. Work on a forceful and coordinated sequence of movements in throwing the javelin. Follow-through will then be possible.

TEACHING PROGRESSION

Teach or work on the following:

grip

release

throwing from a stand

cross-step and throw

approach, or run, and cross-step

approach, cross-step, and throw

approach, cross-step, throw, and reverse.

RULES

- The runway may be unlimited in length, but not less than 98 feet 6 inches.
- The length of the javelin is not less than 7 feet 2½ inches, and the weight should not be less than 5.2 ounces.
- The javelin must be held in one hand in the grip, with the little finger closest to the point.
- An underhand motion of throwing the javelin is illegal and is therefore a foul.
- The trial is not recorded unless it breaks the ground.
- Three trials are allowed in both preliminaries and finals.
- Measure from the nearest mark made by the javelin to the inside circumference of the restraining line.

Class Dicussion of Fundamental Factors in Starting (Bob Young, Honolulu Star Bulletin Photographer).

Part III

TEACHING AND COACHING

General methods and techniques of teaching and coaching are applicable to all physical activities. In this section, their utilization—specifically relating to track and field—is discussed. Chapter 12, which covers teaching methods, includes material for the beginning teacher as well as for the more experienced teacher. Each teacher should be aware of both general and specific teaching methods. In addition, an in-depth method of gathering and planning learning experiences related to track and field is presented; it includes a resource unit, a teaching unit, and a sample lesson plan.

Good teaching is one aspect of good coaching: In Chapter 13, specific information related to a fuller understanding of the principles related to training and competition are included, as well as general strategy for competition. Frequently, training is understood merely as repeated physical exercises. The intent of this chapter, which has been developed for the coach, is to attach a broader meaning and understanding to the term *training.* More specific information concerning suggested training schedules for each event is included in Appendix I.

12

Teaching Methods and Techniques

DESCRIPTION

Track and field offers a stimulating challenge to the teacher. Each event is a new experience; each individual, a new and different personality. The beginning teacher will find that good teaching is a result of adequate preparation and the ability to anticipate difficulties. Some of the more basic teaching methods are included below as a guide in preparing for instruction.

Methods of Teaching

The tasks of teaching track and field events center on helping the learner to create concepts, on directing or leading practice, and on analyzing the learner's movements.

The whole method advocates presenting in its entirety the complete act or a natural subdivision of a large unit. The part method is based upon analysis of the component parts of an activity for the purpose of identifying a logical sequence of parts for presentation from the simple to the complex. The whole method proves generally superior to the part method when a whole is defined as the largest whole, or unified whole-part, which the learner can grasp without undue confusion.

The precise steps in teaching a track and field event by the whole method include

1. establishing concepts

2. providing experiences with the whole

3. analyzing performance

4. providing for practice in parts as needed

5. continuously reanalyzing performance

6. re-establishing whole performance

7. again analyzing

8. again providing for practice in parts as needed

9. continuing analysis

10. again providing for whole performance

Appropriate demonstration procedures for teaching track and field techniques emphasize careful preparation, mastering the technique by the demonstrator, orienting the learner as to the purpose of the demonstration, performing the act correctly during the demonstration, promptly presenting and terminating the demonstration, and providing immediate opportunity for pupils to practice. Loop films, movies, pictures, diagrams, and charts help students build concepts of good performance techniques.

Appropriate explanation procedures for teaching track and field techniques emphasize brevity, pointedness, clarity, meaningful vocabulary usage, and maintaining attention with the voice at a conversational level.

Drill plays an important part in learning. It provides for the repetition necessary to perfect a performance. With careful organization, drills can be meaningful, interesting, and motivating to pupils.

The sequence in learning information and understanding does not vary from learning track and field techniques. Information may be acquired by rote memorization without the pupils' having a functional understanding of it. However, teaching methods should allow for maximum opportunity to apply and practice information in life-like experiences.

Motivation is essential to learning. Learning requires activity on the part of the learner; unless she is motivated to act, no learning can take place. Motivation, though a highly individualized problem, can best be accomplished by such means as helping pupils to understand and accept learning goals, providing opportunity to experience success, and emphasizing rewards rather than punishments. In general, intrinsic motivation proves superior to extrinsic. Information about records and outstanding athletes adds interest, as does the knowledge of average performances for various ages and classifications. As in all learning, progress is a motivating factor. Pupils like to check their performance in competition with others, as well as with their own progress in time and distance. Relays—all-around or pentathlon-type events—add interest to class presentations. However, highly pitched competition with emphasis upon individual winning, appropriate for interscholastic teams, does not fit a class situation since it tends to discourage below-average performers. Group competition, in which each student is given an opportunity to contribute to a group effort, is appropriate for class instruction and for increasing motivation.

Good discipline is necessary for satisfactory progress in group learning and safety. It is conceived as gradually expanding freedom which at no time is greater than the pupils' capacity to handle.

Transfer of learning is essential to effective education; however, because of changes in either the physical or emotional environment, an experience can never repeat itself in exactly the same form. A teacher can increase the likelihood of transfer by understanding the factors inherent in the program.

Methods of presentation may stress formality or informality. Outcomes determine the desirable degree of formality or informality for any learning.

In teaching track and field there is a place for mass, small groups, and individual procedures. The extent of desirable emphasis depends upon the type of activity and upon the situation in which the learning-teaching process occurs. For effective group teaching, group composition should represent a reasonable synonymity of purpose among its members. Groups or squads within a class are particularly appropriate for track and field. When several events are in progress simultaneously, there usually is sufficient activity for all and a minimum of waiting for turns. The teacher should move from group to group, giving help as needed.

Pupil leadership proves essential to a sound pupil-centered program. The basic concept of pupil leadership recommends that all such assignments for pupils provide a real learning opportunity. Student leaders are valuable, especially in large classes.

The values of coed activities can be considerably enhanced by attention to appropriate teaching methods. Carefully selecting activities, adapting rules, using official equipment suggested for boys and girls, and organizing and conducting class or recreational periods serve to increase the likelihood that full advantages of coed participation will be realized.

The foregoing statements related to teaching methods (whole or part, demonstrations, explanations, selection of drills, sequences in learning, motivation, transfer of learning, formality or informality related to presentations, discipline, group composition, student leadership, and coed activities) have been applied to selecting and formulating the units included in this chapter. The resource unit, teaching unit, and sample lesson plan will be highly valuable to the teacher who needs to plan and organize all learning experiences during the track and field unit. The progresssions to follow, content to consider, presentation of materials, setting of drills and performance evaluation, plus information mandatory in excellent teaching are included. For specific information related to executing a particular event, the teacher must refer to the extensive description within the appropriate chapter.

PLANNING UNITS AND LESSONS

A *unit* is a planned sequence of learning activities or experiences which develops into a meaningful whole involving purpose for the pupil and the achievement of significant goals. Units may be classified as either *resource* or *teaching.*

Resource Unit

A resource unit is an accumulation of information useful as reference material for the development of teaching units. It includes general objectives, many ideas for teaching, subject matter proposals, and useful teaching aids. The selection of these materials should proceed from a thorough investigation of pertinent literature and from a careful consideration of teaching needs. The resource unit assures the availability of basic information that will serve for many teaching units with different groups and in various situations. A single teacher or a program planning group may be responsible for its preparation.

Teaching Unit

A teaching unit presents materials and procedures useful for instructing a specific group in a specific situation. Although the teaching unit focuses upon actual teaching-learning needs, it may provide more information than daily use requires, since no one can predict accurately the exact progress pupils may make within a given period of time. The teacher or teacher and pupils cooperatively may plan this type of unit.

Units may also be classified as subject matter (or traditional) on the one hand, and as experience-oriented on the other. The *traditional,* or subject-matter, unit includes a body of logically arranged, predetermined subject matter or skill standards for all to master. An *experience unit* centers about experiences needed for achieving desired objectives and is organized psychologically around pupil purposes. Although the selection of content, organization of activities, and standards for achievement will vary according to these differing types, both kinds of units will use subject matter and include experiences.

The following steps suggest a pupil-centered approach with pupil planning, but may also be useful for a teacher-planned unit.

1. Study the needs, interests, and abilities of the specific pupils for whom the unit is to be used.

2. Prepare proposed objectives and state them in terms of pupil achievement and development.

3. Consider pertinent subject matter and select the most appropriate.

4. Consider limitations imposed by time, facilities, and size of group.

5. Plan approaches and methods for orientation, presentation, practice, analysis, and other appropriate teaching-learning experiences.

6. Consider culminating activities such as exhibits, demonstrations, all-star games, or competition with other classes for inclusion in a unit; these are useful in many situations.

7. Plan for evaluation.

Although the most valid means of evaluating a unit plan would be to appraise actual pupil progress, the persons involved in unit preparation may find help in checking their plans against accepted criteria. Twelve questions are included as criteria for evaluating both the methods of preparation and the completed units.

1. Does the unit grow out of the valid needs and interests of the pupils?

2. Is the experience set in a lifelike context that has meaning to the pupils?

3. Does the unit provide experiences which, while in contact with immediate interests and needs, lead to new experiences and progressive pupil growth?

4. Does the unit lead naturally to new experiences and serve as a motivation for additional learning activity?

5. Does the unit's level of difficulty challenge the ability of the best pupils, but also allow for purposive activity and development for each individual in the group?

6. Does the experience represent the best possible use of time and effort of all concerned to develop desired skills, knowledge, understanding, and attitudes?

7. As a whole, is the experience of value in integrating learning from other areas of the course and the curriculum?

8. Does the unit provide activity of a type that allows for fully realizing the social values of group learning?

9. Does the unit provide for ample opportunity to apply the new learnings to real conditions?

10. Is the unit practical with reference to time available, group size, equipment and facilities available, and pupil maturity?

11. Does the unit provide for a variety of different types of experiences in the total curriculum? Has this type of activity been overused to the exclusion of other possibilities?

12. Does the experience provide for maximum use of exploratory activity and problem-solving?

If a person or group feels that affirmative answers to the above twelve questions apply to a proposed unit, one may confidently expect that a competent teacher will have significant results in learning and development.

Lesson plans help with details concerning objectives, experiences and activities, materials and methods. As a unit is being taught, daily preparation for teaching is necessary to ensure achievement of unit objectives. Although usually prepared for single sessions, a lesson plan may include more or less than one day's activity, depending upon the length of time required to achieve desired or possible ends.

Although the first lesson in a unit should be prepared in detail, specifics for subsequent lessons should be planned only after the previous ones have been taught. The planners may then consider actual progress and focus their teaching upon immediate group and individual needs. Projecting detailed lesson plans too far into the future leads to fixed and stereotyped teaching preparation. Formulating lesson plans shortly before applying them encourages the flexibility needed for helping each pupil progress at his maximum rate.

Equally excellent lesson plans may take various forms. A columnar style may have parallel entries under headings such as Objectives, Activities or Experiences, Subject Matter, Methods, Materials, Correlation with Previous Lesson, Preparation for Next Lesson, and Evaluative Procedure. An outline form presents needed information briefly under appropriate headings; paragraph style allows for description of what the planner or planners wish to achieve and how they propose to do it.

While there is no one "best" form for lesson plans, elements essential for any plan include

1. objectives that are, or can be, made meaningful to the pupils and which are appropriate for the group and individuals involved

2. experiences and activities for the various class members

3. enumeration of materials needed

4. methods and procedures to be used

5. correlation with previous and future plans

6. plans for evaluating pupil progress

7. provision for comments by the teacher at the lesson's conclusion

These evaluations of the lesson's effectiveness should be used to improve future lessons and filed for ready reference.

Resource Unit

A resource unit provides basic materials useful for the development of a teaching unit. The track and field resource unit, presented in detail, shows the kind of general information and variety of ideas that may be helpful source materials for planning a teaching unit in a specific situation. The following sample track and field unit includes proposals and suggestions in the areas of

1. objectives

2. ways of appraising needs, interests, and abilities of pupils

3. ways of increasing interests
4. facilities and equipment
5. safety precautions
6. lead-up games
7. simplified or modified activities
8. teaching events and their skills
9. culminating activities
10. rules
11. evaluating achievement

Resource units might also include a usable bibliography of books, pamphlets, articles, and audiovisual materials. These materials are included in Appendices A and B.

Objectives

Track and field is specifically aimed at refining the basic skills of running, jumping, and throwing. These skills are naturally inherent in many team, individual, and dual sports. Therefore, they are vital to an individual's proficiency of movements when participating in a sport. Also through this refinement, the individual is brought closer to her capacity of skillful movement—not only in sports, but whenever these skills are called upon. The prerequisite conditioning phases necessary to track and field lead to a higher level of physical fitness. Muscles gain tone and strength, cardiovascular-respiratory endurance and efficiency increase, and neuromuscular coordination further develops.

Participation in track and field psychologically affects the self-concept. Track and field is an activity that has enough events to give each individual, regardless of her skills level, the opportunity to attain some degree of personal satisfaction—whether she competes against others or against herself (improves times, distances, and heights). Realizing that one has competed within her physical capabilities is rewarding in itself. Mental alertness, judgment skills, and a general knowledge of how to use the body efficiently are developed.

The events are individual for the main part, yet each person is a member of a team. The significance of individual success thus becomes a part of teamwork. In this way, other social factors such as graciousness in winning or losing, honesty, sportsmanship, and determination also enter the picture.

Track and field is increasing at all levels—from elementary school through college—and this is especially true for females. A teacher's tact and skill in presenting the unit will determine its success and will mold the students' attitudinal outcomes toward the activity. The potential of track and field for the students' benefits and enjoyment is vast. Creating interest and maintaining motivation are extremely crucial to favorable results.

Although this unit is specifically for girls, it might also be applied to a boys' program. Factors such as differences in rate and interest of learning, readiness levels, and sex-related physical characteristics (strength and anatomical structure) will serve as guidelines to modify the unit.

Appraising Needs, Interests, and Abilities

Observe Pupils

Observe situations prior to the unit which involve running, jumping, and throwing. Appraise attitudes and tendencies in order to determine possible motivational techniques. Assess the specific skills exhibited during participation in the track and field unit. Use times and measurements of performance in class. (See section on Evaluation, page 139.)

Examine School Records

Health and physical examination records are of prime importance because they indicate a student's health status. Scholastic and personnel records reveal past and present status. Past performances and experiences may indicate if present capabilities should be explored.

Pre-test

Administer a battery of skills tests to assess abilities. Utilize physical fitness test scores. Through written survey tests, determine knowledge, interests, and attitudes with regard to track and field.

Obtain Information about Pupils

Information about pupils can be obtained in the following ways: holding informal and formal class discussions; conducting a survey of pupil opinions or circulating a questionnaire; observing, during class, attitudes toward the activity and toward each other.

Increasing Interest

On the *bulletin board,* display articles concerning national, international and local events, records in various events, and names of performers. Draw *diagrams* depicting correct form and illustrations of techniques. Post *charts* in the locker room indicating individual or class progress. *Audiovisual aids* (films, slides, film strips) can be kept attractive and appealing if they are up-to-date, colorful, and informative.

A jogging club might be included in the *intramurals program.* *Competition* is a positive means of stimulating the pupils to do their best. Squads or teams may be formed within the class (intraclass). Different class periods might compete against each other (interclass). In intraschool meets, time trials and finals are held for participants in various classes.

Suggest *reading materials* and ask the students to bring in articles for the bulletin board. As a motivational learning technique, *photograph student performances* if camera equipment is available. *Periodic testing* and evaluation sessions are excellent means of measuring progress.

Events should be uncomplicated, lectures brief, and activity unexhausting. Allow for satisfaction, success, and enthusiasm. This calls for teacher tact and skill. *Students advanced* in various events might demonstrate their skills and aid in teaching.

Take the class to a *track meet,* preferably one involving girls. The class should keep a *track and field notebook* of current events, records of performances, printed material concerning forms and techniques, and so forth.

Allow the girls to wear *matching or team outfits* when competing as a team. A *buddy system* sometimes allows students to evaluate each other.

Facilities, Equipment, Supplies

Track and field can be taught with minimal specialized equipment, and a great deal of improvisation is possible with a little effort and ingenuity.

Track

The track should be a 440-yard oval with, preferably, a 240-yard straightaway. Allow for at least six marked lanes, each a *minimum* of 30 inches—but preferably 42–48 inches—in width. Mark relay zones and staggered starts.

An open field may be modified for events such as a "one-lap run," "two-lap run," "half-lap," etc. This will call for measuring the field and setting up standard times.

Starting Blocks

There should be at least one pair of starting blocks per squad. If the school has a wood shop class, ask these future carpenters to construct starting blocks. If starting blocks are difficult to obtain, holes may be dug in the ground to serve that capacity—*provided they are not in the track area.* (The latter is undesirable and the hazards great. Try to avoid.)

Partners may act as starting blocks. Pairs of girls work together: one girl sitting behind the starting line with her feet in the position of the blocks, while her partner practices or uses her for the starts.

Batons

There should be at least two batons per squad. Batons are easy to make. Rolled-up newspapers bound with tape and cut to baton size, mailing tubes, shortened broomsticks, or mop handles serve the purpose very well.

Jumping Equipment

If specialized equipment is unavailable, the following substitutions may be made for the high jump, standing broad jump, and long jump:

1. For the *standards,* modify volleyball or badminton poles.

2. *Crossbar* may be a bamboo pole or a rope weighted with two tennis balls. (Check the bamboo pole daily for splinters or split areas.)

3. *Landing pit* may be made of old mattresses, scraps of foam, other soft materials. Use tumbling mats for the long and standing broad jumps.

4. Mark off a *runway* 85–110 feet long with a takeoff board, if possible, and a foul line.

Hurdles

Low hurdles should be 30 inches high; high hurdles, 33 inches in height. Ask the wood shop class to construct several hurdles, or use rolled up mats. Hurdles can consist of any type of lightweight material that can extend the width and suspend the height of the hurdle. Hurdles must fall when not cleared. Excellent hurdles are:

bamboo poles

string or cord weighted by tennis balls

cut-off broomsticks

yardsticks

Throwing Equipment

Shot put—weighs 8 pounds for girls and 4 kilos for women (8 pounds, 13 ounces)

Discus—can be made of rubber; official weight for girls is 2 pounds 3¼ ounces

Javelin—7 feet 2½ inches

Softball

Basketball

Baseball

General Supplies

whistles, starting gun, starting flags

stopwatches

lime and linemarker

finish tape or string

measuring tape

first-aid kit

record book, roll book, pencils

Safety Precautions

If improvised, equipment should be carefully checked and repaired daily. Replace if necessary. Examine facilities regularly: track conditions (holes, apparatus obstructing the course, etc.), placement of field events, lane markings, etc. Always have the first-aid kit on hand.

To avoid muscle injury, the students must warm up sufficiently before exerting themselves in their specific events.

Insist upon proper dress: correct shoes, properly fitted clothing, clothing suitable for the weather.

Establish ground rules and regulations concerning the use of facilities and equipment.

1. Do not use without supervision.
2. Teach proper use of equipment.
3. Put equipment away after using.

Remind students to remain in their own lanes while running. When not running, move to the grassed area or to the outside of the track.

Since track and field is strenuous, do not overload the student. Allow for adequate rest during the activity. Observe physiological principles and make students aware of them.

1. Warming up is essential.
2. *Keep moving after a race*—no sitting or lying down.
3. Avoid overstretching muscles in warm-ups.

At the beginning, teach proper forms in running, throwing, jumping, and landing. Injuries may be caused by poor or improper techniques.

Follow a proper sequence in the teaching progression. Maximum speed, strength, or force are never needed nor should they be utilized in the early stages of skill development.

Lead-Up

A conditioning program designed to physically aid the student in track and field endeavors is of prime concern at the start of the unit. Prior to the unit, most girls are far from being in condition for the physical requisites of track and field. General conditioning can be presented to the entire class together at one time. This program should consist of stretching, relaxing, and strengthening exercises and participating in speed and endurance-producing actions. Specifically, this calls for jogging, wind sprints, walking exercises, running in place, deep breathing, and vigorous flexibility exercises.

Flexibility is a major objective in conditioning in that it aids in increasing the *range* of motion of the muscles, in preventing muscle injury, and in improving muscle explosiveness. Conditioning is conducive to mental readiness as well.

An exercise series consisting of warm-up activities specific to the events to be covered for the day should be continued throughout the unit prior to each daily lesson. In this way the long-range effects of the conditioning program are maintained and the immediate requisites for the specific events are met.

Modified Activities for Running

Reaction

Lying on their backs, participants should quickly jump up, turn, and run 15 yards in the opposite direction at a command. This aids in keeping the body low during the first few running strides of sprinting.

Foot Flexibility

The students should take off their shoes and pick up marbles or small pellets with their toes. This increases toe flexibility for the clawing action in running and strengthens the arches.

Resistance by Partner

One girl should run 36 yards while her partner holds her hips (waist) from the rear. The front partner lifts her knees as high as she can as she struggles against the resistance. She should run as she would in sprinting, being careful not to lean forward and lower her body to overcome resistance.

Running in a Straight Direction

Runners should attempt to run a straight line drawn on the track or field. This improves their ability to stay in their lanes during all-out sprint efforts.

Running with Toes Pointed in a Straight Direction

Girls tend to rotate their thighs inwardly when running in an all-out sprint. They should run in an all-out effort down a straight line with knees pointed in a straight direction coinciding with the line. The inner edge of the foot should touch the line, not cross over it.

Running for Knee Lift

Practice running with both hands in front of the body, holding palms down at waist level. This aids in developing the proper hip action needed in a race.

Up and Down the Field

Under the guidance of a leader, the girls should run up and down the field in groups of six to eight, going back and forth over a specific area or around the track. The leader signals when to sprint, when to jog, and when to sprint again.

Modified Activities for Jumping

Run-up to Accelerate

Make a 100-foot mark. From a standing starting position, the runner runs as fast as she can to the end of the distance. She then runs this distance in the opposite direction, trying to hit a predetermined mark with her stronger foot.

Run Off a Springboard

With a run-up distance of 40 feet, the performer runs up, springs from the board, and attempts to walk in the air and land with both legs stretched forward fully extended. A double thickness of mats should be placed for landing.

Jump Over a Bar

A takeoff mark is placed 4 feet before the bar, which is 3 feet 6 inches, to 4 feet 6 inches high. In a long jump position, the athlete jumps over a collapsible bar. The landing area is a pit, and the jumper aims for maximum height.

Vertical Jumps

The athlete jumps vertically to see how much height she can attain with an outstretched hand touching a mark on the wall.

Modified High-Jump Height

The girls jump without a bar at first in order to overcome any fear of jumping.

Modified Activities for Throwing

Students should practice throwing to each other, paying attention to throwing the discus, javelin, or ball high and far. To emphasize height, a football goal post can be used as a target to throw over.

Football throws may be used as a lead-up to the javelin throw. For both, use the same action of leading with the elbow. To work on *grip* for the shot put, use a 12-inch softball.

Teaching Events and Specific Skills

Determine the motivational techniques necessary to the unit and to maintaining student interest. See sections related to Increasing Interests. Introduce the unit through class discussions of track and field history (relate to the Greeks and the Olympics), current events and names, and desired objectives.

Teach proper form, frequently reviewing and practicing throughout the unit. Form should be taught from the start of the conditioning program, since the skills begin from that point and then move toward specialization. Periodic skill and knowledge tests may aid in this respect.

Progression follows from learning the basic skills of running, throwing, and jumping into the specialized areas of sprinting and distance running, hurdling, relays, and field events. Within each event, another set of progressions takes place, moving sequentially through the phases of the skill and its execution.

Simple and modified activities allow for drill and practice. Such activities, however, should not postpone too long the beginning of competition. Provide competition as soon as possible. Teams or squads may be formed within the class to compete against each other through any of the following methods:

pupil choice

teacher selection

on the basis of physical fitness tests

counting off

alphabetical arrangement.

Culminating Activities

A track and field unit is best climaxed with a track meet (interclass or intraclass). Such an event adds motivation and interest early in the unit when students are competing to make the qualifying times required for the meet. By limiting the number of events a girl may enter, there are more chances for participation by more people. If possible, the rest of the school may be invited to watch the competition; parents also may be invited. Exhibition events by the more skilled and advanced varsity students may be presented at the meet.

Attend an interscholastic meet. Hold a track clinic for those interested beyond class activities. At a PTA meeting or perhaps the day of the track meet, the students might display their track notebooks compiled from the beginning of the unit.

Rules

The Track and Field Guide, published biennially by the Division for Girls and Women (DGWS) of the American Association for Health, Physical Education and Recreation, is recommended as the guide for official rules and regulations of a track and field unit for girls. (For boys, *The Official Collegiate Track and Field Guide,* published by the NCAA, College Athletics Publishing Service.) *The A.A.U. Track and Field Handbook,* published annually by the Amateur Athletic Union of the United States, contains rules used in national, local, and state AAU meets.

Evaluation of Achievement

As a basis for indicating progress, keep a running record of times and distances of each event. A scoring system may be used to record improvement.

Administer specific skills tests. This may be part of the time trials. Times and distances would serve as an indication of specific skills and abilities.

If a track meet is held, use the final results as possible bonus points, but do not discriminate excessively against those who do not make the finals. Use minimum standards of performance as guidelines for assessing student abilities.

Administer a test on rules and strategy to determine knowledge and understanding of track and field. Observe student attitudes, such as their cooperation and participation during class. Solicit a student evaluation of the program—likes, dislikes, ideas for improvement.

REFERENCES

See the selected Bibliography at the end of this book. For a list of films, see Appendix B. For the names of companies where equipment can be purchased, see Appendix A.

Sample Teaching Unit (Secondary School Level)

This sample teaching unit, prepared with the aid of the preceding resource unit, illustrates a rather traditional type of subject-matter unit plan for the purpose of assisting teachers in their own planning.

SITUATION

Pupils

Thirty-five sophomore girls comprise the class.

Thirty-four girls are capable of physical participation. Since one girl has an asthmatic condition, she has been medically advised to refrain from exhausting activities.

Two girls have track and field experience and are on the varsity girls' track team: One is a hurdler; the other competes in the high jump and long jump.

Facilities and Equipment

open field with a 440-yard oval-shaped track, with a 240-yard straightaway and at least six marked lanes

starting blocks (at least four)

batons (four to eight)

high jump standards and bar

landing pits for high jump, long jump, and standing broad jump

hurdles

shot put, discus, javelin, softball, basketball, and baseball

whistles, and a starting gun or flag

stopwatches

lime and linemarker

finish tape or string

measuring tape

first-aid kit

recording book, pencils, roll book

Time

eighteen periods, 50 minutes each

5 minutes allotted for dressing; 10 minutes for showering and dressing.

OBJECTIVES

To teach and refine the basic skills of running, throwing, and jumping through the following activities:

1. sprints, distance races, relays
2. shot put, discus, javelin, softball, basketball, baseball throws
3. Long jump, high jump, standing broad jump

To contribute to physical and organic development as well as skill and neuromuscular development:

1. muscle strengthening
2. cardiovascular-respiratory endurance development
3. increase total physical fitness
4. improve reaction time
5. increase kinesthetic awareness

To contribute to mental development:

1. judge speed, distance, force, weight, and timing of movement
2. understand track and field techniques

TEACHING PROGRESSIONS

In a conditioning and warm-up program, emphasize proper form in running, throwing, and jumping through the use of the simple and modified activities in the following breakdown:

1. *Fundamentals of running:* sprinting, starts, middle distances
2. *Fundamentals of throwing:* holding the object, preliminary swing, footwork and delivery, release and follow-through
3. *Fundamentals of jumping:* run approach, takeoff, jump, landing

Concentrate on the following specialized skills: hurdling, relays and baton passing, shot put, discus, javelin, long jump, and running high jump.

TEACHING METHODS

Introduction and Orientation

Have a class discussion of track and field history (relate to Greeks and the Olympics) and current sport events (national and local). Show film, if possible. Diagram the location of various events on the blackboard. During the unit, inform the students of safety and ground rules.

Conditioning Program

For the first week, conduct jogging, wind sprints, running in place, calisthenics, and loosening exercises for specific activities. The teacher should observe faulty running form and begin to teach correct form. Vary the program with lead-up and simple modified activities. Again, observe and assess skills.

Skill Drills and Practice

Sprinting

a. Separate the class into the same number of groups as there are lanes on the track. Girls line up in file formation within each lane and practice starts and running dashes. The teacher checks for common faults—swinging arms, not looking straight ahead, leg action.

xxxxxx	X	....
xxxxxx	X	....
xxxxxx	X	....
xxxxxx	X	....
xxxxxx	X	....
xxxxxx	X	....

Start   T (time)

b. Practice starts with brief spurts only. With the girls in file formation, running one after another, the girl who has just run gives out the commands for the next runner.

c. Same as the first sprinting drill above, but mark times for one another.

d. For reinforcement, drill occasionally with simple modified activities for reaction, running with resistance, running in a straight direction, running with the knees pointed in a straight direction, and running holding a stick.

Relays

a. *Stationary Baton Pass.* Arrange the class into squads of equal number, and have them stand in columns. The last girl in each column passes the baton forward to the next girl. They should pass with the left hand and receive with the right, changing hands when receiving the baton. The procedure continues until the front girl receives it; then, the direction reverses itself, and the baton is passed back.

b. *Walk-Through Sequence.* Each girl places herself at a distance 6 feet from the girl in front (preferably in groups of four). The receiver does not look back to receive once she has seen the passer move forward.

c. *Running Exchanges.* Squads of four girls stationed 15–20 yards apart run exchange distance at half-speed. Either speed or distance increases after the girls have learned to smoothly execute a change and to time the takeoff.

Middle Distances

a. The girls jog 220 in small groups rather than individually. They then run 220 in 40-seconds pace time. Repeat several times. Times are called out at 110 during run.

b. Increase the distance to 330 yards, then to 440 yards. Call times at 220 yards or 330 yards. Pace for 440 yards in 85 seconds, 880 yards in 3 minutes. Times should diminish with practice.

Hurdling

a. Use the simple and modified activities for jumping. These drills are good for hurdles.

b. *Walking Beside the Hurdle.* After determining the lead leg, the girl walks with her trail leg adjacent to the hurdle. As she passes the hurdle, she swings her trail leg over the top of the side of the hurdle.

c. The girl walks over the hurdle with her lead leg. As her rear leg comes over, her partner should hold her knee and foot to support and guide it in the proper direction.

d. *Running Through Gauze.* With a strip of gauze taped across the hurdle instead of the crossbar, the girl approaches in a running stride and breaks through the gauze. This increases familiarity with hurdle.

e. The girl jumps over the gauze.

f. The girl jogs to hurdle the gauze and clears it.

g. Run over the hurdle, run to the hurdle and clear it.

h. Flight over the hurdle from the starting blocks.

Long Jump

a. *Run-up to Accelerate.* The girls determine the length of the run needed by running in the opposite direction from the takeoff board. One of them notes the point at which the runner is the fastest; from this point she determines where she must start. Practice sprinting, going through the pit without jumping. The girls should work in groups of four in order to watch each other: One is at the takeoff board, another at the marker, and one is watching the runner's approach.

b. *Running Off the Springboard.* The runner jumps from the springboard and practices the "walking-in-air" motion. She then moves to the takeoff without the springboard. In this exercise, also concentrate on using the arms and check the head's position in the jump.

c. Jump over the 3-foot bar.

d. Practice landing with or without the springboard. Concentrate on landing with both legs stretched forward.

High Jump

a. Determine the better takeoff foot. The girls should take three strides and jump on one foot. Next, follow with a hop over the low bar with one foot and land on the same foot. Follow this by raising the bar and approaching from either left or right at a 45-degree angle.

b. *Kick.* With the bar at a height of about 2½ feet, approach from a definite distance (five to seven strides away). Attempt to clear by 6–12 inches. As the body goes over the bar, kick the lead leg high in air.

c. With the bar raised higher, the girls take a brief run, kick the free leg up, and hop over. As the body goes over, arms reach down toward the takeoff foot; the landing is on the two hands and the takeoff foot. Practice for vigorous kicks, and spring off the ground for height.

d. Working with a partner, the girls determine the length of the approach by watching each other approach and spring. The takeoff should be approximately an arm's length from the bar.

Discus

a. Drill with the basketball throw.

b. *"Bowling."* Four to six girls divide into two groups and face each other; they roll the discus back and forth, stressing correct grip, underhand arm swing, and release off the index finger. The discus should be rolled in a straight line with a good release.

c. Use a horizontal swinging pattern and release the discus at the side and off the index finger while standing. Stand in a "forward" stride, with feet 24–30 inches apart; the right foot should turn out at approximately 45 degrees, and the left toe is on an imaginary line with the heel of the right foot. Emphasize pushing against the right foot, uncoiling the body, releasing, and reversing.

d. *Throw with the Turn.* Concentrate on driving with the right leg, vigorous uplift of discus, speed, and maintenance of balance in reverse.

Shot Put

a. *Stationary release.* Place feet in the position that follows the glide. Feel the shot in the hand, then lift it into position next to the jaw, neck, and shoulder. With the elbow bent and slightly out from the side, push the shot up and away from body. Movement of legs must correlate with arm movement: Bend knees and then extend the legs in synchronization with arms. Push shot away at a 45-degree angle.

b. *Glide Without Shot.* Assume the starting position and execute the gliding action continuously for ten to twelve times repeatedly. Use a large area and do not confine to ring yet. Watch out for hopping. Emphasize the left leg kick for rapid movement.

c. Start in the circle, glide, and release the shot. Draw practice ring circles on the grass, dirt, or sidewalk.

Javelin

a. Drill with softball and baseball throws for distance. Work in small groups and in couples.

b. *Standing Throws with Javelin.* Practice in line formation. The body is at right angles to the throw, and the arm is drawn back. From extended arm position to rear, the pull forward is made with the elbow leading the rest of arm. The release is performed forcefully.

c. *Carry.* The girls stand in two lines, facing each other approximately 20 yards apart. The first girl runs toward the opposite group. Stress proper alignment of the javelin in the carry. The javelin should be above the shoulder and near the top of the head. Run without breaking the rhythm, bring the javelin back to the throwing position, and then return to the carrying position. The girl hands it to her opposite number in the other group, who repeats the maneuver.

d. *Carry and Throw.* The girls line up side by side and practice throwing. Each one retrieves her own javelin after the completed throw.

e. *Approach Run and Cross-step.* The girls line up and, in succession, run the length of the field as if they were running to throw the javelin. They go through the entire sequence of motions, including the cross-step and reverse, but without the javelin. Check carefully for form.

Tryout Activities

After drilling, allow for taking times and measurements. Every capable student should participate in each event. Since discouragement comes easily, allow for some periods of fun. Better results are obtained without concentrated practice and drill.

Informal Activities

Allow the students to select three events of their choice—either two running and one field, or two field and one running. Hold a time trial to establish the "official" class records.

Tests

Conduct skills tests. Rely on minimum standards of performance (see page 222). Give one test immediately after the skills have first been learned. Conduct the same test again at time trials. Note improvement.

Communication and Continuity

At the beginning of each period, outline the activities to be covered. Students should be familiar with the equipment (explanation and manual experience) before starting the event—e.g., hold and examine the shot put, discus, or javelin.

Allow adequate time for explanation, demonstration, and questions of each event. Mainly, use the whole—part-whole method to teach events. Establish teaching stations.

Constant review and practice is necessary. The drill may be limited, but there should be sufficient time for practice and trials. Before dismissing class, briefly mention what will be covered in the next period.

Post informative diagrams and leaflets depicting form and technique in the various events. In the locker room, post a progress chart covering each individual's performance.

Out-of-Class Activities

If supervision is available while equipment is being used, intramurals periods may be used for practice. Jogging clubs are both popular and constructive. Encourage tryouts for the interscholastic girls' track team. Attend local meets.

Organize and participate in extramural track meets with other schools (non-varsity).

Pupil Participation in Planning

Seek pupil suggestions regarding areas of emphasis, team formations, films, or other forms of activity. Keep a bulletin board and class notebook. If the pupils work in pairs or smaller groups, they usually evaluate and help each other. Highly skilled girls can instruct in specific events. The medically excused girl can help by taking times and measurements and recording scores.

The students should be responsible for putting away equipment after each class period. Student leaders might take roll and report absentees to the teacher. Students may conduct their own warm-up routines in squads or in circle formation with the leader in the center.

Planning

Outline daily lesson plans the day before class meets, depending on what activities were or were not accomplished and completed in the previous lesson. Lesson plans will vary in detail and depend on the desired activity (drills, lecture, demonstration, etc.). They should be indicative, however, of time allotments and *specific* objectives to be accomplished.

Teaching Hints

The teaching of skills must be based on an understanding of the principles of movement. A thorough understanding of these will aid the teacher in communicating meaningful and descriptive terms with the learner. It will also aid in analytical procedures during drills and practices. Consult the following section on fundamental drills for the basic mechanical principles related to running, throwing, and jumping.

The number and location of teaching stations will depend on the size of the class. Teaching stations enable supervision of all squads. Allow for rotation from station to station during the class period.

It is best to organize the class in groups of four to six students for drills. An even number enables pairs to work together at times, and the small number per group increases the students' ability to work closely together. Lecture and demonstration should involve the class as a whole; then, divide into working groups for drills and practice at the teaching stations.

Fundamental Drills

In a concern for brevity, the author has not included fundamental drills for the sprints, middle distances and distances, relay racing, discus, and javelin. It seems that one could easily make applications related to the drills for the discus and javelin by observing and following the drills used for the shot put. The hurdle drills and starting drills only need slight adjustments in order to be applicable to sprinting and the distance runs. Chapter 5, related to relay racing, contains very specific drills and formations for relay practice; therefore, that event is not included here. The drill formations included are for the following: starts, hurdles, long jump, high jump, and shot put.

Starts

Grade level: 7 to 12

Suggested time for drill: 15–20 minutes

Playing area and facilities needed: one track

Equipment: six sets of starting blocks

Drill

As shown in Figs. 12.1 and 12.2, the players line up in groups of six. At a signal, the first six students practice starting from the starting blocks and run for about 20 yards. This system is followed until every

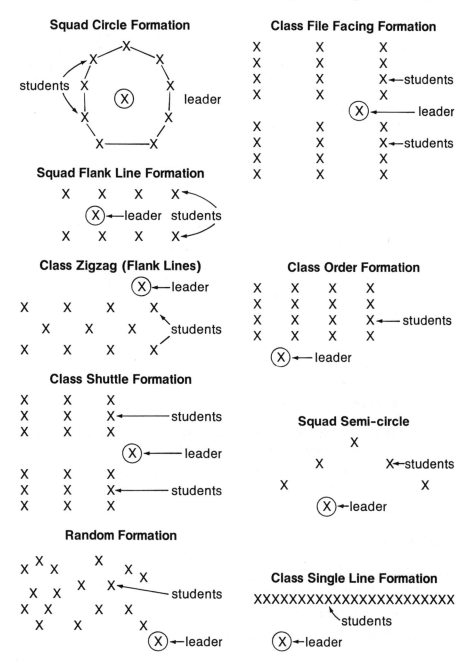

Squad Circle Formation

students   leader

Class File Facing Formation

Squad Flank Line Formation

Class Zigzag (Flank Lines)

Class Order Formation

Class Shuttle Formation

Squad Semi-circle

Random Formation

Class Single Line Formation

XXXXXXXXXXXXXXXXXXXXXXXX

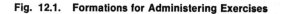

Fig. 12.1.   Formations for Administering Exercises

student has had a chance to practice starting. After the proper techniques in starting have been explained, on the proper signal six students assume a set position at the starting blocks. The signal is given to start, and the students run about 20 yards, leave the track, and return to the end of the lane they came from. While the first group is returning, a second group starts. Continue this process during the entire drill. The teacher makes individual and group corrections and suggests methods for improving performance.

Some drill variations are as follows:

1. With a smaller group, use one lane and teach students one at a time.

2. If starting blocks are unavailable, dig holes in the track (at the end of the straightaway where they will not mar the track).

3. Time runners for the 25- and 50-yard dash.

4. For starting, use either a starting gun or clapper board (slap together two boards to make the sound of a gun).

Safety Considerations

1. Students must wear shoes.

2. Warm up before practicing.

Teaching Hints

1. Demonstrate and teach the activity to the entire class before assigning students to specific squads.

2. In starting, move at half-speed until the students have thoroughly mastered the fundamentals and are ready for full speed starts.

Hurdles

Grade level: 7 to 12

Suggested time for drill: 10–20 minutes

Playing area: one football field

Equipment: thirty hurdles, twelve starting blocks

Drill
As shown in Fig. 12.4, three women line up along the end zone on two sides. At a given starting signal the first student in line jumps over the

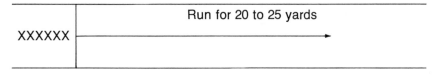

Fig. 12.2. Squad or Group Formation for Starting

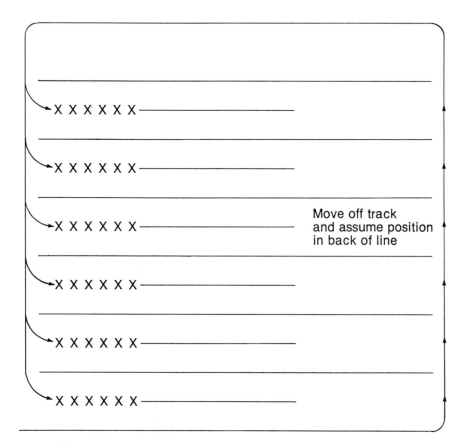

Fig. 12.3. Class Formation for Starting

hurdles. This process continues as the students take turns running and jumping over the hurdles. (For the distances to the first hurdle and distances between, see Chapter 6.) Nine lines of hurdles can be used on one football field.

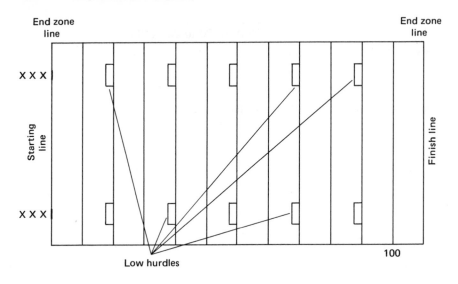

Fig. 12.4.   Squad or Group Formation for Hurdling

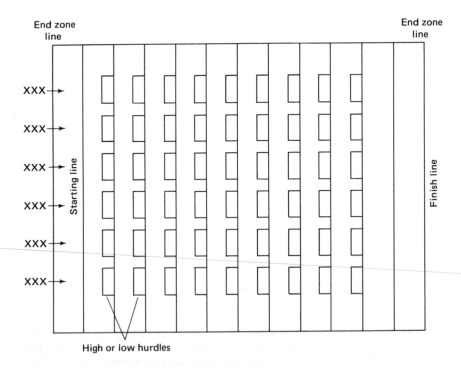

Fig. 12.5.   Class Formation for Hurdling

Drill

After the hurdles have been placed at the correct positions on the field and the first student is assigned a position to start from the starting blocks, a signal is given and the student runs 120 yards and jumps the five hurdles set on the course. The students take turns, and the best times for everyone are recorded each day.

Some drill variations are as follows:

1. Emphasize competition between students on both time and races.

2. Use fewer or more hurdles for the drill.

3. Advanced students in the upper grades should jump high hurdles.

4. Assign two squads to practice hurdling.

Safety Considerations

1. Place hurdles on the field so that the base (legs) face the starting line.

2. Do not permit students to wear track shoes.

Teaching Hints

1. Practice with only one hurdle, and then add hurdles as students become more skillful.

2. Require students to wear shoes.

3. Require students to use proper techniques. At the beginning of this unit, stress form and proper techniques rather than speed.

4. Teach the entire class the proper techniques of hurdling before assigning students to squads.

Long Jump

Grade level: 7 to 12

Suggested time for drill: 10–20 minutes

Playing area and facilities needed: four long jump pits for four squads

Equipment: four steel tapes, four rakes

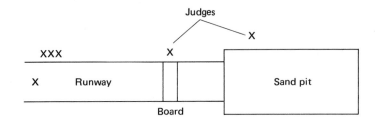

Fig. 12.6.   Squad or Group Formation for the Long Jump

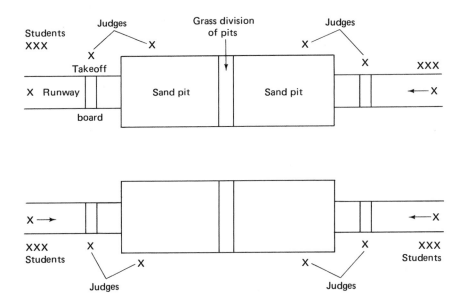

Fig. 12.7.   Class Formation for the Long Jump

Drill

As shown in Fig. 12.1, six students are assigned to the long jump area. One student jumps; two measure and judge the jump; and three participants, waiting for their turn to jump, stand in line at the beginning of the runway. As shown in Fig. 12.2, six students are assigned to each of the four areas if four long jump pits are available.

While one student runs down the runway to jump, a second student moves to the runway to get ready for her jump. Two students judge, measure, and record the jump. Students should rotate positions so that each has an equal opportunity to practice long jumping.

Some drill variations are as follows:

1. Practice the standing broad jump.
2. Practice trial runs to the takeoff board.

Safety Considerations

1. Keep the runway clear.
2. Judges should give a signal for each student to start down long jump runway.
3. Track shoes should not be worn.
4. Rake prongs should always be facedown on the ground, away from the long jump pit.

Teaching Hints

1. Teach the techniques and fundamentals of long jumping prior to squad practice.
2. In long jumping, emphasize the importance of speed, takeoff, and height.
3. Do not try to break a record each time; rather, work on basic fundamentals at half-speed. Try to emphasize single fundamentals and then bring them all together.

High Jump

Grade level: 7 to 12

Suggested time for drill: 15–20 minutes

Playing area and facilities needed: two high jump pits with shavings

Equipment: four high jump standards and two crossbars, inflated inner tubes, foam pieces, sawdust for landing area

Drill
Students can practice various types of jumps. Raise the crossbar as they improve.
Each squad leader should keep records, and each person's best performance for the day should be recorded.
Some drill variations are as follows:

1. Use one jumping area for as many as six students.
2. Approach the crossbar from any angle.

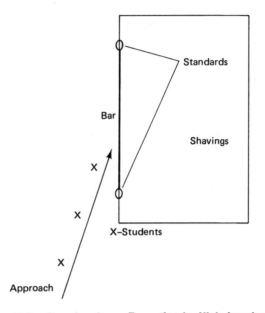

Fig. 12.8.   Squad or Group Formation for High Jumping

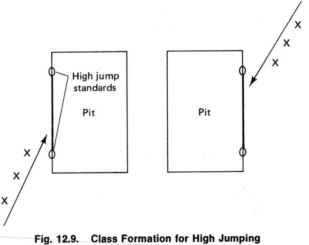

Fig. 12.9.   Class Formation for High Jumping

3. Students can practice the drill without the crossbar and work on form only.

Safety Considerations

1. Clear the area before the second student jumps.

2. Wear gym shoes rather than track shoes.

3. Be sure there is an adequate supply of loose shavings in the jumping pits.

Teaching Hints

1. Demonstrate the activity to all students before assigning them to squads.

2. Check student records and see that they are in the team captain's possession.

3. Make individual corrections and suggestions for improving performance during the activity period.

4. Explain, demonstrate, and practice the proper techniques in the Eastern and Western rolls and straddle jump.

Shot Put

Grade level: 7 to 12

Suggested time for drill: 10–20 minutes

Playing area and facilities needed: shot-put area, shot-put circle, fencing around shot-put area

Equipment: two 8-pound shots, two 12-pound shots, four softballs

Drill
As shown in Fig. 12.1, one student is in the shot-put area and five students are outside the area awaiting their turns to put the shot. The shot-put area is fenced off for safety reasons.

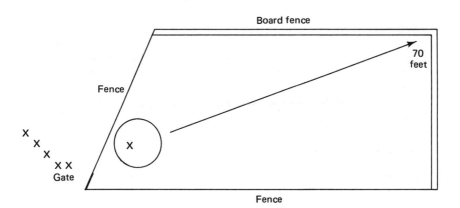

Fig. 12.10.   Squad or Group Formation for the Shot Put

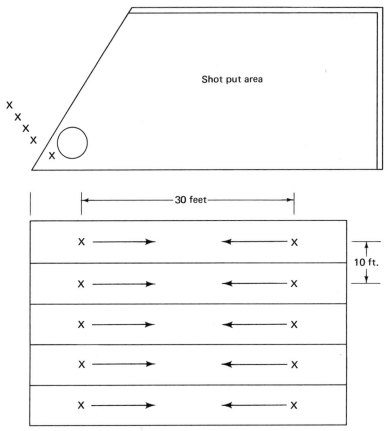

Softball shot put area

Fig. 12.11.   Class Formation for the Shot Put

Drill

As shown in Fig. 12.1, one student is in the shot-put area. After she puts two shots, she retrieves the shot puts and takes a position at the end of the line outside the area. Other students in the line follow the same procedure.

A variation for this drill is to practice shot put outside the shot-put area with softballs.

Safety Considerations

1. Only one student at a time should be permitted in the shot-put area.

2. Emphasize the importance of safety practices in this activity.

Teaching Hints

1. Until the fundamentals are learned correctly, practice with softballs.

2. Demonstrate the safety procedures used in this activity.

3. Practice shot put without going into step movement, and gradually add specific fundamentals as specific skills are learned.

TIME DISTRIBUTION

Allow one day for introductory film and orientation; one day for film loops of various events; three days for conditioning program. Continue these exercises throughout the unit.

Allow two days for skills testing; three days for time trials; two days for written tests (one pretest with discussion and one final).

Allow one day for an intraclass tritathlon track meet. The remainder of time should be spent on teaching, drills, and practice. Time distribution will depend on class progress.

EVALUATION

Evaluation is based on skills tests, time trials, and the progress chart. Teachers and students should hold brief discussions regarding progress (time permitting). The teacher should observe

attitudes

cooperation

sportsmanship

participation

Points given for performance are based upon Point Scores Used in the Evaluation of Track and Field Performances (table in Appendix D).

Sample Lesson Plan: Relay (Nonvisual Pass) (Secondary School Level)

This is one example of the kind of lesson which can be planned as an outgrowth of the preceding teaching unit.

CLASS

Sophomores

SIZE

Thirty-five students (one medically excused because of asthmatic condition)

GOALS

General Objectives

To develop a sense of judgment and timing.

To incorporate a sense of team competition within track and field.

To encourage cooperation and dependence in teamwork.

To add enthusiasm, interest, and variation in the running events.

Specific Objectives

Behavioral

To teach and have the students perform nonvisual baton pass correctly and successfully.

To introduce the different relay races, especially the difference between the sprint, distance, and medley relays.

To teach the specifics of the exchange zone.

To provide warm-up exercises for general conditioning and specific activity.

To remind students of the consequences of improper dress.

Conceptual

To understand the criteria for a fast and successful baton pass.

To understand the exchange zone in relation to the baton exchange and the runners.

To realize the importance of placement of runners.

FACILITIES, EQUIPMENT, SUPPLIES

batons—minimum, two per squad of eight

grassy area at least 100 yards in length

oval-shaped track approximately 440 yards long, with at least 240 yards of straightaway and with lanes and exchange zones marked off

whistles

stopwatches

starting blocks

first-aid kit

roll book

SAFETY PRECAUTIONS

Insist on proper warm-up and stretching exercises. Check the track for holes, dangerous terrain, or any other obstacles. Always have the first-aid kit on hand.

Avoid the following dangerous conditions when passing the baton:

1. After passing the baton, the runner should remain in her own lane to avoid possible interference or collision with an incoming or outgoing runner in another lane.

2. The student must learn to time the takeoff with the incoming runner to prevent the incoming runner having to overreach and perhaps collapse in an effort to thrust the baton forward, or to prevent a collision between the incoming and outgoing runners due to faulty timing.

3. After receiving the baton the runner stays close to the left of the lane to allow room on the right for her teammate.

4. Be sure that runners are in the correct lane.

Remove starting blocks immediately after the start, and caution the girls to check the track for runners before crossing it when they are not participating.

TEACHING PROGRESSION

Explain and demonstrate baton pass mechanics.

Practice baton pass skill: stationary pass, walk-through pass, and running pass on grassy area.

Explain exchange zone.

Practice running pass in exchange zone.

Actually run the 440-yard relay.

CLASS MANAGEMENT FOR A 50-MINUTE PERIOD

Allow 5 minutes for *dressing.* While students dress, check out equipment with gym attendant. Meet students on the field, and make note of those who are tardy.

Allow 1 minute for *roll call.* Students should be organized into four squads of eight people each in single file, side by side. The squad leader heads each squad and faces the teacher. (T=*teacher;* L=squad leader; X=students):

```
                T

L           L           L           L
X           X           X           X        T = teacher
X           X           X           X
X           X           X           X        L = squad leader
X           X           X           X
X           X           X           X        X = students
X           X           X           X
X           X           X           X
```

The leader of each squad checks to see which *members* are *absent* and reports to the teacher. Leaders should also observe and report those students not dressed in track and field uniform or those improperly dressed. Send absence slips to the office.

Allow 2 minutes for *announcements.* If some students have not been dressing for class, remind them that this is equal to a minus mark. Accumulating too many minuses will result in failure in the course. If time trials are scheduled for the school's varsity track team for the afternoon, those interested should be urged to go and watch. It will provide a fine opportunity to watch some proficient baton passing.

Allow 5 minutes for *warm-ups.* Squad leaders step out and lead the class in the exercises the teacher calls out. Squads remain in formation. Exercises are as follows:

jumping jacks—20

alternate toe touches—20

side benders—20

deep knee bends—10

leg lunges—20

forward kicks—20

wind sprints—2

Return to squad formation

Allow 7 minutes for *teacher demonstration and explanation.* Students sit on the floor in squad formation. If necessary, ask them to move for a full view of the teacher.

Select four students to aid in the following demonstration:

TABLE 12.1 TEACHING TECHNIQUES

Activity	Explanation	Organization
Stationary pass	1. Last person hold baton. 2. With the left hand pass to right hand of person in front. 3. Second person receives baton with right and puts it into left hand. She passes to third person in same manner. So on until last person receives baton. 4. Repeat, reversing direction.	Four students lined up, one behind the other X—X—X—X
Walk-through pass	Same as above	X—X—X—X Students space themselves further apart and walk through sequences.

Questions and answers

Drills and Practice: 10 minutes

1. Stationary pass	Same as above	Students stand in squad formation and practice pass.
2. Walk-through pass	Same as above	Students divide squads of 8 (2 teams of 4 each). Drill as in Demonstration.
3. Running pass	Students now run and pass. Repeat sequence until students can execute a smooth pass.	In teams of 4, students space themselves approximately 25 feet apart.
4. Pass within the exchange zone.	Explain the zone: 1. The zone is 20 yards long. 2. The baton must be handed to the succeeding runner within this zone. Students practice the pass in the zone, timing their takeoff with the incoming runner.	Students form semi-circle around one of the zones. There are eight teams. Two teams are stationed at each of the zones on the track.

Allow 10 minutes for the *culminating activity.* Answer questions concerning any of the foregoing explanations or demonstrations. Put the eight teams into two heats of four teams each. While one group runs, the other will help in timing. Those not timing will act as critics of the baton passes.

Run two heats of a 440-yard relay. Take the times and record on the progress chart. Upon dismissal, the students must collect equipment and return to equipment room.

Allow 10 minutes for *shower and dressing.* The teacher checks that the dressing room is in order before students leave. Are any showers still running? She collects stray articles and deposits them in the equipment room. She does not allow students to wander in the hallway before the bell rings.

EVALUATION

The teacher observes the students' performances, noting whether explanations and demonstrations were understood. Also note which areas must be reinforced or cleared up next period. The teacher informs the students as to their performance during drills and practice (corrects errors, reinforces good form, etc.). Note student comments.

TEACHER COMMENTS

Note which students seem to work well together. Repeat the material related to the passing zones. If the students could have had more fun, put in one fun-type relay for the next class. Talk to . . . concerning her general apathy.

Track Offers a Stimulating Experience for All Age Groups (Bob Young, Honolulu Star Bulletin Photographer).

13

Coaching Methods and Techniques

GENERAL TRAINING PRINCIPLES

Training is frequently understood merely as repeated physical exercises. The intent of this section, which has been developed for the coach, is to attach a broader meaning and understanding to the term *training*. More specific information concerning suggested training schedules for each event is included in Appendix I.

In drawing up a training schedule, the following basic principles borrowed from the pedagogical sciences must be observed and understood:

all-around development

awareness

gradualness

repetition

individualization

All-around Development

This includes harmonious development of the muscles and motor qualities (strength, speed, flexibility, and agility); the excellent work of the cardiovascular, respiratory, and other systems and organs; the diverse ability to plan and coordinate movement; high moral and cultural standards, and strong will power.

Awareness

Awareness means that every person must know the *what, why, and how* of all she does. The athlete must accumulate a large reservoir of knowledge and experience, and use it appropriately before she can possibly train effectively and be successful in competition.

Gradualness

Gradualness means that the training burden should progress gradually but consistently. The volume and intensity of training must also increase gradually.

Repetition

Repetition is based upon the physiological principle that repeated efforts are required for forming conditioned reflex ties, and for corresponding changes, reformation, and improvement in the organs and systems and their functions under the influence of training. Without repeated physical exercises, there is no development and improvement.

Individualization

This principle proposes that the individual's abilities (age, preparedness, the development of her different qualities, etc.) must be taken into account by those engaged in training her.

Adhering to the principles of training, a general schedule might consist of a long-range program, a yearly program, a seasonal program, or a class unit. The selected program should depend upon the degree to which one wishes to pursue excellence. The long-range plan is based upon the principles of gradualness and individualization. At the present time the basis of many years of training is the repetition of approximately the same annual program, but with a steady increase in the value, quality, intensity, and complexity of training with every passing year. Planning for a four-year term—from one Olympiad to the next—is often the course.

The determining factor for effective training and success is the year-round program (eleven months a year). This eleven-month cycle is divided into three periods or seasons:

preparatory

precompetitive

competitive

Preparatory Period

This stage emphasizes most effective techniques for developing the general qualities of strength, endurance, flexibility, and agility needed to perform the event. It usually lasts no less than five months—five to seven sessions a week for preparing the more advanced performer, three to four sessions for the novice. Near the midpoint of the period, more concentration is spent on developing event techniques or skills.

Precompetitive Period

This season lasts for about three months. The main emphasis is geared toward mastering a technique while still pursuing practices to bring about the specific endurance and strength needed for the event. It involves contest participation, but only for training and control purposes which will enable the athlete to evaluate her progress and develop the psychological preparedness necessary for the success.

Competitive Season

The competitive season is climaxed by a major championship meet at the school, state, national, or international level. Minor contests are held weekly for the purposes of analyzing movement, performance under conditions of stress, becoming knowledgeable about opponents, and experiencing variations affecting performances.

Regardless of the length of the training program, specific weekly cycles must be established. For noticeable results in performance, three should be the least number of training sessions per week. (The more accomplished athlete has five or six.) Two sessions a day are often conducted in middle-distance and distance training. Each session must be entirely different in order to be beneficial.

During the early preparatory period, the weekly cycle might include:

overdistance work—Mondays, Wednesdays, Fridays

strength training, underdistance, flexibility, and agility work—Tuesdays and Thursdays

(Overdistance work is longer than the required distance.)

During the late preparatory period, more emphasis might be placed upon alternate days of developing and learning technique.

Repeat the training cycle without change for no less than one-and-a-half to two months in the preparatory period and one month in the other two periods. After that, introduce a new cycle. Retain the aim, but vary the means and methods while increasing the volume and intensity of work.

DEVELOPMENTAL FACTORS IN TRAINING

Endurance: To develop cardiorespiratory efficiency.

Fartlek

Fartlek is Swedish for *speedplay,* or running various distances at various speeds. The term *cross-country* also describes the work-load. Women usually work at developing the ability to run up to 10 miles, although longer distances need not necessarily be detrimental. The author is not aware of any outstanding female who trains at a greater distance in one session.

The middle-distance runner must concentrate most of her training program on the cross-country method of training, with an average number between twenty-one and seventy miles run per week. The novice can begin with a 1-mile jog each day and gradually build up to a relaxed run at greater and greater distances.

Interval Training

Interval training is a run on a flat surface on the track. It involves four factors:

1.   a given distance
2.   the number of times it is run
3.   the pace at which it is run
4.   the recovery interval of walking or jogging.

Any one of these four can be considered the gradual measure of progress while the other three remain unchanged. For example, pace, recovery, and distance can be held constant and the number of daily practices or repetitions gradually increased. This is the primary emphasis during the preparatory period. During the pre-competitive season, recovery time lessens with the other factors held constant. The emphasis is upon increasing the pace during the competitive season.

Interval training is recommended during the preparatory season. For sprinters, the number of repetitions are less than the competition distance.

Women training for the half-mile or mile have included the following intervals in their training:

Distance	Progressions in Repetitions	Time/Sec.	Rest/Time
440's	3 to 10	.80– .67	6–3 min.
220's	4 to 15	.38– .28	3–1 min.
880's	2 to 4	3:00–2:25	12–6 min.

The least number of repetitions and rest time, coupled with maximum pace time, is usually undertaken by the novice who is gradually building up to maximum workloads. Pace time is determined by the time of her maximum speed at that distance. The woman who runs her fastest 220 in 28 seconds would start about 10–12 seconds slower—38–40 seconds for a 220 interval. She builds up to about 5 seconds slower than her fastest time. Thus, her 220 maximum load schedule might be 10 X 220's at 33 seconds with a 1-minute rest.

The determining time for starting the quarter begins at 20–22 seconds slower, building up to 10 seconds slower than the fastest. The half-mile time interval starting time would be about 40 seconds slower than the runner's fastest time, and gradually decreases to 20 seconds slower than the fastest time.

Strength

Force times speed is the underlying basis of power. Muscles develop in size and strength when they are overtaxed. This is the implication involved in the overload theory. Strength can be developed through the process involved in formal overload: weight training, isometric contractions and calisthenics, functional overloading which involves overloading the activity itself. In this case, the sprinter would wear weighted boots or a jacket while running, and the high jumper would use weighted boots while practicing the high kick.

Weight Training

Many negative feelings are frequently generated when weight training is mentioned. Namely, the female will develop bulky muscles. *This is totally untrue.* A woman will never develop bulky muscles, because she lacks the male hormone *testosterone* which aids the male in developing a muscular appearance. Modeling and weight-reducing or figure control salons commonly use weights in their programs.

Essential Information for Female Weight Trainers[12]

Before proceeding to lift weights, a person should be familiar with safety factors, proper procedures, principles, techniques, and methods. A thorough medical checkup by a physician is recommended.

Grips

The hand grips are as follows:

1. pronated—palms against bar
2. supinated—palms against bar with back of hand away from body (reverse of the pronated grip)
3. alternated—hands in opposite grips, one up, one down.

Stances

The seven stances are as follows:

1. Basic—back straight, head well up, legs hip-width apart, feet pointing straight ahead
2. squat-legs are bent from standing position until hips approach floor
3. split—one foot in front of body and one foot behind, thus lowering the height of the body
4. crouch—legs and back both bent, resulting in head being closer to floor and in front of body
5. dead lift—should be avoided by all female track and field competitors
6. prone position—lying facedown on floor
7. supine position—lying on back on floor

Movements

The movements are as follows:

1. curl—any movement in which one part of the body is brought closer to another; it is called flexion
2. extension—any movement that is the reverse of the curl
3. press—the slow, continuous movement of extending legs or arms
4. clean—lifting the bar from the floor to the chest-rest position without stopping
5. jerk—similar to the press, but done explosively; legs, body, or other muscular aids are used
6. snatch—lifting a weight from the floor to straight-armed overhead without stopping.

Training Routine

This should be done with the aid of an instructor unless the participant is experienced. There should be three or four workouts per week with rest periods in between. The length of the workout varies with the individual, but usually 30–40 minutes of exercise with a pause only to let the heart return to a normal beat between exercises and to catch the breath suffices. Warm-ups are essential; regular track exercise warm-ups are sufficient. Weight, height, all body measurements, increases in weights, repetitions, and sets should be recorded. Chart the number of times an exercise is performed without stopping. The number of repetitions done with a rest between each set of repetitions are part of the record.

Length of Training Period

Usually about three months of preparatory work and two months of precompetitive work suffice. This will vary depending on the length of the track season. Track women usually should be taken off the weight training schedule at the beginning of the track season. Distance women might continue to use weights during the season if they have shown improvement as a result of tying weights to their legs, body, etc. Field women might use weights for the entire season, with emphasis on quick explosive action during the competitive season.

General Weight Training Exercises

All women track and field athletes will benefit from the following exercises:
high chins or pull-ups
curls
squats
side arm and leg raises
forward bends
sit-ups on incline boards
shoulder shrugs
toe raises
body rotations—standing and sitting
lying on side legs raised
straddle-hops
leg raises
leg curls
back extensions in prone position

Specific workouts for participants in various events are included in Appendix F.

Isometric Exercises

Isometric exercises have a number of advantages over conventional forms of exercise in that time expenditure is very modest and space needs are negligible. A series of isometric exercises can be executed in a minimal 5 minutes whereas most other forms of exercise would require not less than 15 minutes to achieve noticeable results. These exercises may be done with a partner, alone, or using any object that will remain stable at the required height. For example, parts of the stands on the track field can be used. Each exercise should be done three times for 6 seconds each, with a 10-second rest period after each. Recommended isometric exercises are presented in Appendix G.

Calisthenics

Calisthenics are exercises that can be used as a part of the warm-up as well as performed for specific or general strength development. Recommended calisthenics are listed in Appendix H.

STRATEGY FOR COMPETITION

This section is devoted to the strategy of preparing for competition in a track and field meet. Strategy related specifically to each event is described at the end of each chapter covering the particular event.

Top Condition

Top condition is the *most fundamental prerequisite* for the participant in track and field. Top conditioning is achieved by following a well-planned and organized training program that provides maximum physical development as well as mastering techniques and skills related to the event. Generally, the demands of the event will dictate which physical components need to be emphasized during the training period—strength, endurance, speed, power, flexibility, etc. The means and methods of attaining these are presented earlier in this chapter.

Identify Variables

Identify the variables which are present at a competitive meet and devote one practice session per week to either working under or discussing similar conditions. Some of the variables are:

types of surfaces for running, jumping, and throwing

climatic conditions such as rain or clear, hot or cold temperatures, low or high altitudes

time of competition—morning, afternoon, evening

rules and the different order in scheduling events

Make certain that all these variables are considered in several practice sessions. Approximate the time between each event and trial, and warm up. Take the same care that would be accorded in the meet to prevent fouling or false starts. Take the same amount of rest between each trial as at the meet. Practice in competitive shoes and uniform.

Know Capabilities and Weaknesses

Photograph the students who are executing the techniques of the event. Study and evaluate these photographs. Know which warm-up techniques are best for the particular event and the individual athlete.

Self-Confidence

Develop self-confidence and self-sufficiency. The athlete should have a kinesthetic awareness of (feeling for) executing her skills. She must be able to evaluate her faults and be able to work alone. Although the coach should never withhold her sympathy and support, the individual athlete constantly works at and directs herself toward self-reliance.

Eating Habits

Determine premeet eating habits. Athletes should know which foods digest easily and learn how soon they can eat before a contest. If the competition is to last all day, they should know at what time to eat again and what foods.

Personal Items

Anticipate problems involving personal items that might arise during the competition to the detriment of performance. Women's vanity affects their game. If they feel that they are not looking their best, they may fail to do their best. Extra personal items which might prevent embarrassment—such as sanitary supplies, needle and thread, hair ribbons, and combs—are part of the equipment and should not be forgotten.

Check Equipment

Check all equipment prior to the meet and competition. Do not wait until arriving at the meet to change the spikes in shoes (suppose a spike is lost). Check the implement's weight in advance to see that it meets official specifications, as a favorite implement might be the wrong weight. Check the starting blocks, and bring a hammer in case it is needed. Bring a marker and tape for the approaches.

Information in Advance

Know not only the time of scheduled events, but also get advance information about the composition of heats or flights and the number of qualifiers for finals. If there are so many competitors that flights (competing groups) are used in the field events, try to be placed in the best flight. If qualifying for finals is based upon time, try to get into the fastest heat; otherwise, run the fastest possible time. Know the number of qualifiers for semifinals and finals. Sometimes a runner assumes that the top three are qualifying when she is running fourth. This might lead her to decide that she cannot qualify and therefore to slow down, thus permitting another runner to pass her at the tape. She might then find that four were being qualified and had she given her all, she might have made it.

Follow these general procedures for additional preparedness before, during, and after competition:

1. Walk around the area and pay close attention to uneven terrain, hazards, bankment of the track, etc.

2. Stay in the shade until it is time to warm up.

3. Keep abreast of last-minute changes in the time schedule or temperature and weather conditions.

4. Avoid "psyching yourself out" by watching others warm up. Let them watch you.

5. Try not to allow the opponents to detect weaknesses or nervousness. Everyone competing is nervous.

6. Observe the opponents' weaknesses and strategy.

7. Evaluate performances to gain insight on personal improvement. Again, photographing performances is helpful. Ask, was the warm-up too soon, or not enough? Was there adequate preparation for the start, jump, or throw? Was there too much left at the end? Were the throws or jumps consistent? Were performances at their best? Was the pace correct? Was there too much fear of fouling? Was there too much fear or tenseness to allow for a *best* performance?

Correcting these faults during practice will pave the way to better performance at the next meet.

Part IV

ORGANIZATIONAL AND ADMINISTRATIVE FACTORS

Improvised Weight Room. (Bob Young, Honolulu Star Bulletin Photographer)

14

Attire, Facilities, Equipment, Supplies

ATTIRE

Wearing apparel should be color-coordinated and compliment the figure. Running shorts and top are preferably made of a light knit to allow for unrestricted movement. Although not mandatory, warm-up suits are needed on cold or rainy days, or during meets when waiting for events to start. A bra should be comfortable and give maximum support. Panties should be fitted at the crotch and thick enough to absorb perspiration. If a girdle is required, it should be of the lightest material and must not be tight around the thighs. (Carefully selected running shorts might eliminate the need for a girdle.)

Give careful consideration to proper protection of the feet. Preventing injuries and extreme discomfort is much easier than correcting them.

In selecting footwear remember that the shoe must not be too large and cause rubbing or friction—nor too tight, to cause pinching. It should give the proper support at the sides, ball of the foot, and instep.

The novice can wear tennis shoes—especially during the warm-up—but there must be a thick cushion for the ball of the foot; they should also be flexible enough not to restrict foot action. Wear light-weight cotton socks to absorb perspiration, fit snugly to prevent rubbing. Chamois pushers are adequate substitutes. The type of leather used should be flexible so that shoes fit like expensive kid gloves. Shoe tips should touch the large toe but not cramp it. Try on shoes without socks, for they will eventually stretch.

The surface on which the shoes are used will determine whether indoor shoes with rubber soles or spikes are needed. The event will determine where the emphasis of support should be— that is, high-on-the-toes sprinting action requires four-spiked shoes whereas ball-of-the-foot heel action for distance running requires spikes spread wider on the soles plus a small rubber heel or sponge. Another factor is the throwing surface or approach area for field events. Many athletes wear sprinting shoes and protect the heels with a cup, rubber heels, or felt. Others use the *one-spike heel.* On concrete surfaces indoor rubber-soled shoes which support both the heels and the balls of the feet are best. Spiked shoes should have removable spikes. A drop of oil in each hole before putting in the new spike will prevent rusting.

A more advanced runner will possess the following:

a pair of warm-up shoes

a pair of practice shoes

a pair of meet shoes

practice uniforms—sweats, running top, pants

meet uniforms—sweats, running top, pants

OFFICIAL EQUIPMENT AND SUPPLIES

Excellent and well-preserved equipment, facilities, and supplies add much to track and field performance. If there is no track field available, ask permission to use the nearest one. Most coaches or teams do not mind if their facilities are used, provided they are properly cared for, not abused, and usual practice is not interferred with. The use of these facilities will save much time and expense in attempting to lay out a plan for the field events, runways, and passing zones, etc. Jones[17] includes excellent sections related to planning facilities. The DGWS *Track and Field Guide*[2] includes the specifications for facilities and equipment to be used in the women's program.

FACILITIES

The track is approximately the same width at all points, permitting eight to nine individual lanes. The track is 440 yards in length and oval-shaped. Each curve and straightaway is approximately 110 yards, although there are acceptable variations.

All field events are laid out in the infield so that all field events may be held simultaneously. If necessary, warm-up runways, pits, and rings are located between the two straightaway legs. Long-jump pits are approached by runways from two directions. The high-jump runway is not less than 59 feet in length. The javelin runway is not less than 98 feet 6 inches in length, and 13 feet 1½ inches in width.

The running track and field event runways, circles, pits, and landing areas are often several inches higher than the adjacent level of the field to provide drier conditions in wet weather. Many runways are now made of Grasstex or Tartan surfaces.

There are two separate rings for meet competitions in both the discus (8 feet 2½ inches) and shot put (7 feet in diameter). The pole lane will often be used for distance events only. Both the dash and hurdle races will be held in the lanes farthest away from the pole. At this time the Tartan track is the very best available. The 3M Company (see Appendix A) can supply more information. Stands are placed 25 feet from the track parallel with the straightaway.

EQUIPMENT

Equipment should meet the official specifications used for women. (See AAU *Track and Field Handbook and Rules* or DGWS *Track and Field Guide.*) Here is a brief list of the equipment needed:

high jump standards and metal crossbar

aluminum batons

hurdles 30 and 33 inches high

shot puts—8 pounds for girls and 4 kilos (8 pounds 13 ounces) for women

discus—inside rubber for women or outdoor (2 pounds 3¼ ounces)

starting blocks

javelin—aluminum (to minimize breakage) or wooden, 7 feet 2 inches in length, weighing not less than 1 pound 5.2 ounces

concrete elevated shot-put circle (diameter, 7 feet) and toeboard (4 feet long on the inside, 4½ inches wide, and 4 inches high)

takeoff board for the long jump (4 feet long and 8 inches wide), set in the ground close enough to the pit to make possible a jump of 11 feet and make the pit; will enable even the slower learner to make the pit on each jump

concrete elevated discus circle (diameter, 8 feet 2½ inches) with sectors forming an angle of 60 degrees at the center of the circle

When purchased from reputable dealers, equipment will usually be quite durable, even lasting beyond normal use. Most companies include information related to the care of the equipment.

Take the following precautions in preserving facilities and equipment:

Secure a canvas for the landing pits to protect the surfaces from rain and strong winds—especially for the sand pits in the long jump. Also secure a canvas for the shot-put and discus circles.

Discourage athletes from using long spikes on asphalt areas.

Store equipment in a secure place that is neither damp nor extreme in temperature. Do not allow holes to be dug on the track. Use the shot put only in the specific area set up for it. Put away all movable equipment at the end of the season. Use a long chain and lock on the hurdles to prevent them from being stolen between practices. Clean the starting pistol frequently. Record all equipment and supplies given to each person and have them sign for each piece.

Stopwatches should be allowed to run down after each practice. This takes the pressure off the spring mechanism when it is not in use. Slip the watches into individual protective pouches to minimize crystal breakage. Secure the watch to a long cord around the neck while timing.

Improvising Equipment

Limiting official equipment and supplies need not curtail the program. Starting blocks can be made out of two blocks of wood. There should be a long spike in the bottom of each to nail it into the ground. Two blocks of wood without spikes can be used in the gymnasium. Glue a strip of rubber to the bottom to prevent marring the floor; a participant sits on the ground behind the blocks with her feet behind each block to prevent movement as the runner backs into them and leaves them.

Improvise jumping standards by using volleyball or badminton standards. Drill holes 2 inches apart starting at 3 feet in the pole and insert two long spikes at each height to hold the crossbar.

The top of the hurdle can be made out of string stretched between two objects 30 or 33 inches off the ground. Draw the 7-foot shot-put circle with chalk. Use inflated inner tubes covered by a canvas in the high jump pit to soften the landing area.

Use mats to soften the landing for indoor long jump pits. Masking tape sufficiently wide to meet official specifications can serve as the takeoff mark. Check before each jump so that it does not cause tripping.

For strength, conditioning weights can be made out of plastic bottles filled with sand. Mark the weight on the outside with fingernail polish. (See Part IV opening photograph.)

A whistle or two boards clapped together can serve as the starting signal. Lanes, starting lanes, and finish lanes can be made of removable tape. Use cut-off broomsticks as batons for relays. Knitting yarn may be used for the finish tape.

SUPPLIES

accurate stopwatches to note time in minutes, seconds, and tenths of seconds

lime and linemarker

steel tape measures, 100 and 200 feet

starting gun and shells (22-caliber for practice, 32-caliber for meets)

wood shavings or foam rubber pieces for high jump pit

sand for long jump pit

rake

broom

finishing yarn

pencils, paper, and clipboards for recording performances

first-aid kit including adhesive tape, medication for cuts and bruises, elastic bandages, foot pads

15

Organizing a Track
and Field Meet

A Games Committee is frequently in charge of organizing a track
and field meet. Such a committee comprises

meet director

ticket manager

program editor

head groundsman

public relations director

These individuals try to ensure a successful meet as a result of
their preparations. They also provide an adequate announcer during
the meet and follow through on postmeet responsibilities.

MEET DIRECTOR

The meet director is the chairman of all the committees. All her
planning and preparation for the track meet should start at least 6
months to a year in advance. This is the person who

1. works out details related to the meet
2. plans track and field layout
3. informs schools and coaches of the events
4. selects officials

Before working out details, the meet director first selects the
place to hold the meet. In considering this aspect, it is wise to note

track conditions, parking, publicity, locker space, seating capacity, and transportation. The field's availability must also be considered. In general, high school competition occurs once a week. Major meets (championship) are usually conducted on the weekend, while dual events can be held in the middle of the week.

Always select the *place, date,* and *time* of the meet *early* to avoid scheduling conflicts. The boys' track team may already be scheduled to host a meet there, and you may need to select a different day. Also reserve alternate dates in case of bad weather.

Events and Time Schedule

Events and time allotted for each are usually standard, having been set through tradition. The following events are usually found in an interscholastic meet, with the order and suggested time listed[2]:

HIGH SCHOOL AFTERNOON MEET

Time	Distance	Event
4:00	hurdles (50-yard, 70-yard, 80-meter, or 100-meter)	shot put
		high jump
4:15	880-yard run	
4:30	100-yard dash	
4:45	440-yard dash	discus throw
5:00	220-yard dash	running long jump
5:15	1500-meter run or 1-mile run	
5:30	440-yard relay	softball throw
5:45	880-yard medley relay or 880-yard pursuit relay	

COMBINED GIRLS AND OPEN TRIALS (ALL-DAY MEET)

Time	Distance	Event
	TRIALS	
9:00	hurdles—girls	
9:20	hurdles—open	
9:40	100-yard dash—girls	
10:00	100-yard dash—open	shot put—girls
		high jump—girls
10:20	220-yard dash—girls	
10:40	220-yard dash—open	

Time	Distance	Event

SEMIFINALS

Time	Distance	Event
11:00	440-yard dash—girls	discus throw—open long jump—girls
11:15	440-yard dash—open	
11:30	hurdles—girls	
11:45	hurdles—open	
12:00	100-yard dash—girls	softball throw—girls javelin throw—open
12:15	100-yard dash—open	
12:30	220-yard dash—girls	
12:45	220-yard dash—open	

FINALS

Time	Distance	Event
1:30	hurdles—girls	shot put long jump—open
1:40	hurdles—open	
1:50	880-yard run—girls	
2:00	880-yard run—open	
2:10	100-yard dash—girls	
2:20	100-yard dash—open	
2:30	440-yard dash—girls	discus throw—girls high jump—open
2:40	440-yard dash—open	
2:50	220-yard dash—girls	
3:00	220-yard dash—open	
3:10	1500-meter or 1-mile run—girls	
3:20	1500-meter or 1-mile run—open	
3:30	440-yard relay—girls	softball throw—open javelin throw—girls
3:40	440-yard relay—open	
3:50	880-yard medley relay—girls	
4:00	880-yard medley relay—open	

After deciding the details, the meet director informs the schools and coaches of the schedules at least four or five months in advance. Entry forms, together with information sheets, should be sent at least three weeks before the meet. These entry forms include

1. schedule of events

2. number of events a person can enter

3. rules

4. location of meet

5. deadline for returning entry form

6. data on housing, eating facilities, and directions to track field (if applicable)

Equipment and Supplies

The meet director is responsible for seeing that official equipment and supplies are available (see page 184). The following supplies must be added to the list on page 187:

scoresheets

finishing yarn

batons

drinking water

discus (2 pounds 3 ounces)

hurdles

javelin board and javelins (7 feet 2¼ inches, weighing not less than 1 pound 5.2 ounces)

judges' stands

towels

whistles

starting blocks

official rule book

crossbars

softballs

shot put—8 pounds (girls), and 8 pounds 3 ounces (4 kilos) (women)

long jump board (4 feet 8 inches wide)

When planning the track and field layout, the meet director works closely with the *groundskeeper* to determine the placement and markings of all field events, and the starts and finishes of the track events.

Placing the judges' stand must also be done in advance to prevent later problems. They might do a better job if positioned away from the curb, but placing them this way can interfere with field events inside the track. Ideally, judges should be stationed on both sides of the track.

Safety Precautions

In addition to their other responsibilities, the meet director and groundskeeper must draw up plans to provide for maximum safety to both participants and spectators. In regard to the field, some safety suggestions are as follows:

1. No holes on track.
2. Jumping pits should be made with material that will permit a soft landing. Spade these areas constantly during the meet.
3. Rope off discus, javelin, and shot put areas. These events may cause injury to a spectator, judge, etc. Only allow participants inside.

OFFICIALS

Selecting officials is one of the most difficult yet most important duties of the meet director. Officials should be chosen at least three weeks in advance of the meet. First, the meet director must decide how many officials will be needed. This number may vary according to the size of the meet. Most authorities suggest approximately 59 officials for a championship meet:

1 referee

1 starter

7 finish judges

5 inspectors

5 timers

3 clerks

1 walking judge

24 field judges

3 marshals

1 scorer

1 announcer

1 doctor

1 surveyor

1 recorder

1 press steward

1 inspector of implements

1 custodian of numbers and prizes

and 1 photo-finish clerk

Seeding or Scratch in the Meet

In some places, the names of the final starters are delivered to the Games Committee, which then arranges the heats and lanes; the results are then sent to the coaches for final approval and corrections. In other places, a meeting of the coaches, or seeding committee, is held at least three days before the meet to draw and seed the contestants. In this case, the following procedure would most likely be followed:

1. Scratches of entries and added entries are made in each event.

2. Number of preliminary heats is determined on the basis of actual competitor number, number of lanes, and number of contestants desired in the final or semifinal races.

3. Heat leaders are agreed upon and assigned by lot to the various heats.

4. A second, third, or fourth round of contestants, evenly matched, is selected and assigned to the heats by lot. One way is to list the ability or ranking of the women in order from top to bottom. In the case of three heats, the lineup would be

	Heat One	Heat Two	Heat Three
Contestants			
	1	2	3
	2	5	4
	3	8	9

5. Competitors from teams having several entries are assigned by lot.

6. Remaining entries are placed in heats by lots.

Lanes in the meet are also determined by lot. But in the semifinals and finals, the heat winners are usually in the center lanes. The meet director should remind the officials two days before the match, check the PA system, and check the equipment.

HEAD GROUNDSMAN

The head groundsman is in charge of preparing the track and field, equipment, and the facilities. He works closely with the meet director in all his duties. Specific measurements are clearly identified in both the AAU and DGWS *Guides* and, therefore, must be adhered to in preparing the area.

TICKET MANAGER

The ticket manager is in charge of preparing and distributing the tickets for the event. If there are special, season, or complimentary tickets, they should be distributed early. Distribution should be done in a businesslike manner by charging them out to student salesmen. Set up a definite policy regarding those who may receive complimentary tickets.

The visiting school should also have tickets made available to them in the advance sales or distribution. The ticket manager should make adequate provisions for selling and taking tickets at the contest. (Adults usually serve in these capacities.)

PROGRAM EDITOR

In an athletic contest, informative programs for the spectators can raise the event's significance. In most instances, these programs may be free of charge. Advertisements secured for the program often help to defray the printing cost. If programs must be sold, the booklets must be attractive enough to ensure a profit. They must be accurate and complete and contain an official reference for all meet records (and other relevant performances). Not only should complete factual material be included, but also articles, pictures, and stories related to the meet.

PUBLIC RELATIONS

The public relations person's most important duty is to welcome incoming athletes and their coaches. The local alumni of each competing institution assume the role of hosts for their own team and may arrange a special welcoming committee to give a tour of the city or other scenic attractions, and to throw a banquet or party after the meet.

The "p.r." person is responsible for all activities pertaining to furthering public interest and fostering goodwill toward the meet. This does not include those activities directly related to the press, radio, or television. Efforts in the public relations area are limited only by this person's own ingenuity and energy, and by what the Games Committee might consider appropriate and dignified. Projects can be infinite in number. Some examples follow.

1. Make special efforts to contact luncheon and service clubs, as well as other groups, to show movies of previous meets or competing athletes, give talks, and/or sell tickets.

2. Organize premeet parades involving nonathletic groups.

3. In the case of big meets, paid advertising in the newspaper, in streetcars, on posters, in periodicals, and in display windows is effective.

4. Encourage downtown stores to feature track pictures, trophies, and mementoes in their window displays.

5. Find social organizations or groups who would be willing to make a meet a focal point around which to stage a weekend party or overall celebration.

In the case of a very large meet, a publicity director may be needed; in most cases, however, a public relations person should be able to handle the various activities involved.

RESPONSIBILITIES DURING THE MEET

Officials should report 30 minutes before the meet begins. They should already know what duties they will perform. In general, the duties of each official should be as follows[2]:

referee—interprets and enforces rules

starter—must get the women to start together; he gives the command and fires the gun with at least 2 seconds in between

inspectors—report infractions to referee

timers—time winners; usually three official watches plus an unofficial one, in case one of the other three fails *judges of finish*—select all winners; one judge for each place

clerk—keeps running events on schedule or moves them for each place

chief judge of field events—keep field events on time

judges of field events—run off events in accordance with the rules; also run them in time

marshal—keeps spectators out of the area

announcer—keeps everyone informed on the progress of the meet

A good announcer is very important. First, she should be stationed properly: not too far from the field, and not in the announcer's booth used for football games; station her at trackside, whether it is in the first row of bleachers or at a table on the infield.

The announcer will need a supply of basic tools. A working or call sheet will instruct her as to when an event will occur and also when to call up the athletes for each event. For example, the call sheet may read, "1:45—first call for shot put and long jump." This is important because the athletes must warm up before their particular event to minimize the chance of injury.

Communication is an important aspect of a meet. If possible, there should be equipment such as a walkie-talkie or relay telephone. If unavailable, station messengers at the track or field to bring messages to the announcer concerning lane assignments, winners and their times, current leaders in the event, or a progress report from the scorekeeper.

A good announcer should inform the spectators of the standing team scores and the point total needed to win the meet. She should not talk too much or too fast, and be able to create suspense and a spirit of enjoyment.

POSTMEET RESPONSIBILITIES

After a game is completed, the Games Committee is usually left with the following responsibilities:

1. pay officials, if necessary

2. return all equipment; run down stopwatches to take the pressure off the spring mechanism, and place in their protective pouches to prevent breakage; place canvas on landing pits

and shot put and discus circles; clean and store all equipment in a place with no extreme temperature or dampness

3. ticket salesperson reports to ticket chairman concerning contest receipts

4. general financial statements due within a week after each meet

5. concession reports

6. list officials' names, games in which they worked, the date of meet, a rating for each based on state rating plan, and a few remarks about each official's work

7. coaches usually make participation records shortly after each game for award purposes

8. use large envelope as a filing unit for contest data: game and official contracts, all correspondence concerning contest, school and newspaper clippings referring to game

9. thank-you notes to all individuals or groups who helped in any way to make the meet a success

10. release results to the press, radio, and television

16

Officiating Techniques

QUALITIES OF A GOOD OFFICIAL

Officiating at track and field events demands much more than just knowing and interpreting the rules. Listed below are some of the qualities of a good official.

1. Be familiar with track and field rules as outlined in the current DGWS *Track and Field Guide.*

2. Be able to make prompt, just, and accurate decisions about many complex questions and situations.

3. Keep temperament in check. Be courteous and objective at all times.

4. Concentrate on the *immediate task* involving the event, even though other events are scheduled simultaneously

OFFICIALS FOR A MEET

The number of officials necessary for conducting a meet varies. Dual meets will not require as many officials as larger meets. For maximum efficiency, the following officials are suggested for meets where three or more places are being awarded:

1 meet director

1 track referee

1 field referee

1 starter

7 finish judges, including chief

7 timers, including chief

6 inspectors

3 field judges per event, including chief

1 custodian of equipment

1 clerk of course

1 marshal

1 scorer

1 announcer

1 doctor

1 surveyor

1 recorder of new records made

1 custodian of awards

Assistants may be provided for the clerk of the course, scorer, marshal, announcer, chief timekeeper, and chief field judge. No official should act in a dual capacity, nor should any track team manager act as an official at a track and field championship meet.

General procedures for officials include the following:

1. Be sure of date, time, place, and assignment.

2. Inform meet director 24 hours in advance if appointment cannot be kept.

3. Arrive at the track 30 minutes before the meet is scheduled to start.

4. Wear appropriate skirt, white blouse, and tennis shoes.

5. Report to the person in charge of the event. If in charge of the event, check off the other officials as they report.

The DGWS and AAU Track and Field *Guide* books include a more detailed list of duties and responsibilities for each official. These techniques and duties should be studied by officials for the efficient execution of their jobs. The following information is a resume of the more important points needing emphasis. (*Note:* Detailed responsibilities of the following officials were included in the preceding chapter: meet director, marshal, surveyor, custodian of equipment, custodian of awards, announcer, recorder, and scorer.)

Track Referee

Prior to the meet, place competitors in heats. Table 16.1 may be used in forming heats for dashes, relays, and hurdles. Determine the number of heats by the number of contestants and number of lanes available. When past performances are known, determine the fastest girls and place them in different heats. When times are not known, place contestants in any heat; try not to place them against a team-mate in the same heat.

See that all rules are observed, and decide any technical points that arise during the meet. If there are no set rules covering a dispute, *the track referee shall have the final judgment in the matter.*

Take charge of all running events and bear responsibility for properly carrying out the track program. Inspect the proper marking of the track. Confer with track officials to see that each has sufficient personnel. Inform the head officials of the number of heats and the number of competitors who will qualify for the semifinals and finals. After the meet, inspect, approve, and sign the scorers' records.

Clerk of Course

From the track referee, obtain the name and number of all competitors in their respective events and heats. Supervise the drawing of each lane prior to each trial event if the track event is being run in lanes. Make sure each competitor is in her proper lane. The lane closest to the curb or pole shall be numbered "one." Line up runners several heats in advance if there are a number of heats to be run in any event.

Obtain the names and numbers of all qualifiers for semifinal and final heats from the scorer, and make sure that the list has been certified by the track referee. Place each competitor in her assigned lane for the semifinals and finals. If a competitor who has qualified in a preliminary trial withdraws from the competition in the semifinals or finals, no substitute may replace that competitor.

In relay races, check runners against the original entry blank. If a school enters more than one relay team, each of its teams should have a different letter—e.g., blue A, blue B. See that batons are ready for the lead-off runner.

Suggestion: Before the start of each race, it is recommended that the clerk of the course give the head finish judge a card with the names of the starters, their numbers, and the lanes in which they are running.

TABLE 16.1 FORMING HEATS FOR DASHES, RELAYS, AND HURDLES

FOR SIX LANES

No. of Entries	No. of Heats	No. Qualifying	No. Semifinal Heats	No. Qualifying	No. in Final
1–6	0		0		6
7–12	2	3	0		6
13–18	3	4	2	3	6
19–24	4	3	2	3	6

(25 or more require quarter-finals following above pattern)

FOR SEVEN LANES

No. of Entries	No. of Heats	No. Qualifying	No. Semifinal Heats	No. Qualifying	No. in Final
1–7	0		0		7
8–14	2	3	0		6
15–21	3	4	2	3	6
22–28	4	3	2	3	6

(29 or more require quarter-finals following above pattern)

FOR EIGHT LANES

No. of Entries	No. of Heats	No. Qualifying	No. Semifinal Heats	No. Qualifying	No. in Final
1–8	0		0		8
9–16	2	4	0		8
17–24	3	4	2	4	8
25–32	4	4	2	4	8
33–40	5	3	2	4	8

(41 or more require quarter-finals following above pattern)

FOR NINE LANES

No. of Entries	No. of Heats	No. Qualifying	No. Semifinal Heats	No. Qualifying	No. in Final
1–9	0		0		9
10–18	2	4	0		8
19–27	3	3	0		9
28–36	4	4	2	4	8
37–45	5	3	2	4	8
46–54	6	3	2	4	8

(55 or more require quarter-finals following above pattern)

Assigning lanes for semifinals and finals is based on the times of the qualifiers. For races run on a straightaway, the fastest girl is placed in center lane; second fastest, in lane to her right; third fastest, in lane to her left. The other girls are placed from right to left according to times until each lane is filled. The two outside lanes contain girls with the slowest times.

For races on a curve, the two inside lanes contain girls with the two fastest times, the third lane contains the girl with the third fastest

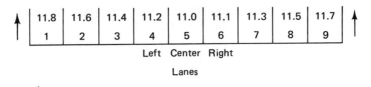

Left   Center   Right

Lanes

↑ Denotes the direction of the run

Fig. 16.1.   Lane Assignments Based Upon Qualifying Times

time, and so on, until all lanes are filled. Place the girl with the slowest time in the outside lane.

Starter

Use a 32-caliber gun and blank shells. Rule on all questions concerning the start. Issue instructions to each heat of competitors about the signal for starting—"On your mark," "Get set," wait approximately 1.7 to 2.0 seconds, and fire the gun. Make certain all competitors' hands and legs are behind the line.

Be the sole judge of anyone making a false start. Before the start of the race, warn all competitors that anyone making two false starts will be eliminated from that race. Assume a position 10 feet from the starting line to the side of the track which is in clear view of the timers.

In races where competitors start on a staggered start or uneven line, stand so that the distance between the starter and each competitor is approximately the same. Signal the timers and judges

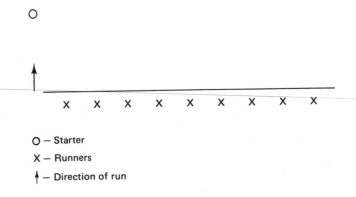

O — Starter

X — Runners

↑ — Direction of run

Fig. 16.2.   Starter's Position in Races Run on a Straightaway

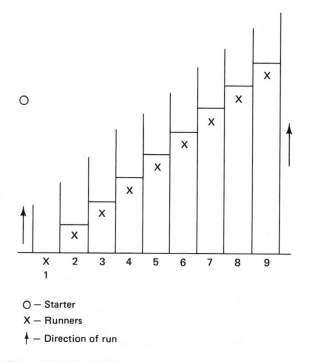

O — Starter

X — Runners

↑ — Direction of run

Fig. 16.3. Starter's Position in Races Beginning with a Stagger

when the runners are ready (before the command "Take your marks" is given). On the command *"Take your marks,"* hold the gun down at the side with firing pin pulled back. *"Get set"* or *"Set"*—raise gun over the head so that the timers will have a clear view of the smoke when the gun is fired. "Get set" is not given until each competitor is completely still. The gun is not fired until 1.7 to 2.0 seconds has elapsed.

Chief Finish Judge

Make certain each judge has a sharp pencil. Have extras available. Ask a messenger to carry slips to the scorer. Properly instruct judges and designate the places to be picked by the other judges.

When the starter blows her whistle, see that all judges are ready and report to the chief timekeeper. Note the finish of each contestant in order to issue a decision in case of a disagreement between judges. If there is a tie in any heat, competitors shall both qualify if lanes or positions are available. If not, the tying competitors shall compete again for the available lane position. Make arrangements to place the judges of the finish and the timers on elevated stands at a minimum distance of 20 feet from the edge of the track.

Before the start of each race, it is recommended that the clerk of the course give the head finish judge a card with the starters' names, numbers, and the lanes in which they are running. At the race's conclusion, the chief finish judge writes the names of the winners on this card in the order in which they finished. Then, she signs the card and hands it to the head timer, who records the times and hands it to the scorer.

Finish Judge

Prior to each event, mark the finish slips with the name of the event and heat numbers; initial, and leave only the competitor's name and number to be filled in at the finish of each race. Stand on the side of the track directly opposite the finish line.

At least two judges should be assigned to each place to be picked, and serve on opposite sides of the track. The finish judge watches the race until the competitors are within 15 to 10 yards of the finish line; he then concentrates on the finish line. If picking third place, it helps to count mentally while focusing on the finish line. Look straight across and count "one, two, three" as the runners cross the finish line.

Pick the competitor at the moment any part of her *torso* (including the neck as distinguished from the head, arms, legs, or feet) reaches the nearest edge of the finish line. A runner who falls before reaching the finish line will not be considered to have finished until her entire body is across the finish line.

Upon completing each heat, fill out the finish judge's slip and immediately turn it over to the chief finish judge. Do not discuss the outcome of the race with other judges until after the judges' slips have been turned in.

Chief Timekeeper

Be sure all watches are numbered and record the name of the person using each watch. Synchronize watches before assigning to timekeepers. Test by touching the stems of the two watches together to start and stop them. Check to see that the stopping times are the same for each watch. If the two watches are synchronized, then one of the two watches should be used to test the remaining watches.

See that the timers are ready, and notify the starter to start the race. Call "Gun is up" to notify timekeepers and finish judges that the starter is starting the race.

Rule on the official time as follows:

1. If there are three watches on one place and all three watches show different times, the chief timekeeper considers the middle time as official (*not* the average of the three).

2. If two of the three watches are the same and one is different, the time in which the two are identical will be official.

3. If there are only two watches on a place with each showing a different time, the slower of the two will be considered official time.

If a second place time is faster than the first place time, consider the second place time to be wrong and adjust the time accordingly. If a decision cannot be made, the chief timekeeper shall confer with the track referee. Have timers clear their watches after the times have been recorded.

Collect all timers' slips after each race, and arrange in order—first, second, third, etc. Send to the scorer. Remind timekeepers to rewind their watches periodically during the meet.

Timekeepers

To become familiar with the type of watch, check the watch before the start of the meet. Before starting each event, mark timers' slips with the event, heat number, and won initials. Then, fill in the time immediately after the race. Timers' slips should be immediately turned over to the chief timekeeper. There should be no discussion with the other timekeepers.

Timing Techniques

Hold the watch lightly in the right hand with the index finger on the stem. (The index finger must have full freedom for movement.) Practice starting and stopping the watch until you get the feel of the stem's action. When preparing to time, take up the slack (extra movement) in the stem by pressing it until the slightest extra movement will start the watch. Squeeze the stem slowly, as in triggering a gun. Only the index finger moves. Take the time from the flash of the pistol to the moment that any part of

Meet _____

Date _____

Place _____

Event _____

Competitors	Organization	Trials									Finals									Best Performance	Place
		1		2		3					1		2		3						
		ft	in	ft	in	ft	in				ft	in	ft	in	ft	in					

Place Winners

Head Field Judge _____

Field Referee _____

Official Scorer _____

Fig. 16.4. Sample Score Card for Discus, Shot Put, Javelin, and Long Jump

the body (torso) of the competitor reaches the nearest edge of the finish line.

After the watch has been started, the timer should watch the race until the runners are 5 to 10 yards from the finish line. At that time, she should focus her eyes on the finish yarn and, finally, press the "stop" button as the contestant's chest contacts the yarn or torso crosses the finish line.

For races of one mile or less, the timing should be to 1/10 of a second.

Inspectors

There should be six inspectors, including the head inspector. The inspector's duty is to report all irregularities to the head inspector and the referee. The referee decides if rules have been violated. In hurdle races, and dashes, two inspectors should stand behind the starting line. The others are placed at intervals along the track.

In relay races, inspectors should be placed to cover each passing zone. (See Fig. 16.5.) For races in lanes around turns, assign an inspector to two lanes for the entire turn with the responsibility for seeing whether or not the runners remain in their respective lanes.

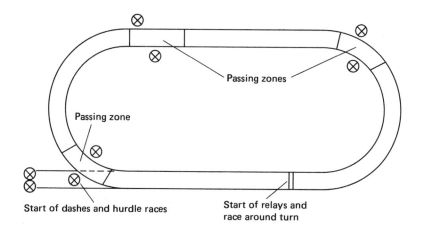

Fig. 16.5.   Suggested Placement of Inspectors

Field Referee

The field referee is in charge of all field events and for properly carrying out the field event program. Determine the order of competition before the day of the meet. Possible methods of conducting competition particularly in the throwing events or long jump are as follows:

1. Each contestant has one trial in the first round, one in the second, etc.

2. Contestants have two successive trials in the first round and one in the second.

3. Divide contestants into flights. Those in one flight complete all preliminary throws or jumps; next flight does the same.

Make certain all field judges and assistants know and understand their duties, method of measuring, and what constitutes a foul in that event.

Head Field Judge of Each Event

See that the equipment is available—implements, measuring instruments, markers, rakes, crossbars, powdered resin for takeoff board. Each judge inspects her own area. Call off contestants' names in order of competition as follows: "Brown up"; "Smith on deck"; "Jones in the hole."

To watch for fouls, stand in the following positions:

1. *Shot put, discus, and standing long jump*—stand to the side of the performer.

2. *Running long jump*—stand beside the takeoff board and focus eyes on the jumper's feet, in relation to the outside edge of the takeoff board. Call a foul if it occurs.

3. *Javelin, basketball, and baseball throws*—stand at the scratch line or arc. Call a foul if it occurs.

4. *High jump*—stand beside one of the jumping standards. In the high jump, announce misses, "First miss," "Second miss," "Final miss." Announce the starting height and subsequent heights to which the bar is raised.

After jumps, signal to the assistants to rake the pit. When pit is in order, announce the next contestant. In the high jump, wait until the bar is replaced and be sure it is still and not shaking in the wind.

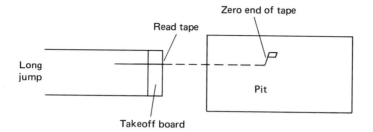

Fig. 16.6.   Techniques of Measuring Long Jump Distances

The order of competition in the finals is usually the reverse order of performance in the preliminaries—i.e., the one with the best throw in the preliminaries should be the last one to throw in the finals. Advise contestants as to runways, sectors, and scratch lines; order of competition, number to qualify for finals, etc. Make sure that contestants who are competing in other events understand they are to report back to their field judge as they finish participating in the other event. Running events take precedence over field events.

Read and record measurements. (See Figs. 16.6 and 16.7.) Measurements for the shot put and long jump should be made immediately after each throw or jump. Record distances under 100 feet to the nearest quarter-inch and, if over 100 feet, to the nearest half-inch below the distance covered. (Ignore fractions less than a quarter- and half-inch.)

1.   *Shot put, discus, javelin:* Measure from the nearest mark made by the fall of the implement to the inside edge of circle circumference along a line from mark of implement to center of

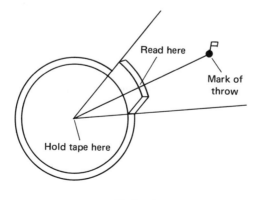

Shot put

Fig. 16.7.   Techniques of Measuring Shot Put Distances

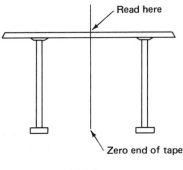

High jump

Fig. 16.8.   Techniques of Measuring High Jump Heights

circle. Hold the zero end of tape at the mark of the implement. (See Figs. 16.7, 16.9, and 16.10.)

2.   *Baseball and basketball throws:* If thrown from a scratch line, measure from the nearest mark made by the implement to the inside edge of the scratch line at the center of the scratch line. Hold the zero end of tape at the mark of the implement.

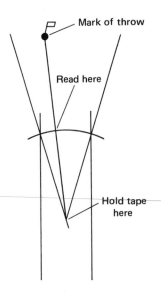

Javelin and Softball

Fig. 16.9.   Techniques of Measuring Javelin and Softball Distances

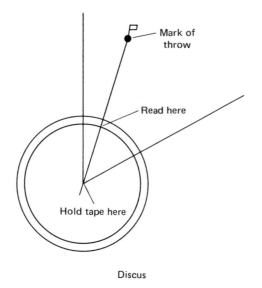

Discus

Fig. 16.10. Techniques of Measuring Discus Distances

3. *Long jump:* Measure from the nearest mark in the pit made by any part of body or limbs to edge of takeoff board nearest the pit. Hold the zero end of tape at break in pit. Use a knife or pencil through the metal loop of tape. Stretch tape at right angles to the takeoff board or its extension. (See Fig. 16.6.)

4. *High jump:* Measure in a perpendicular line from the lowest point on the top side of the crossbar to a point on the same level as the takeoff. Measure the crossbar's height each time it is raised. (See Fig. 16.8.)

Determine who will throw in the finals (one more than in places awarded).

Field Judge

In the throws, keep an eye on the implement and immediately mark the spot where it first touches the ground. Do not retrieve the implement until the throw has been properly marked. In marking throws (not shot put), sticks or pegs can be used. If the second throw is obviously greater than the first, the first marker may be taken up. If a girl's second throw is obviously less than her first

RUNS OR HURDLES

DATE _____   MEET _____

_____ SCORER

CONTESTANTS	SCHOOL	LANE POSITION	ORDER OF FINISH	TIME

Fig. 16.11.   Sample Meet Card for Running Events and Hurdles

RELAY RUNNING EVENT

DATE _____   MEET _____

_____ SCORER

CONTESTANTS	SCHOOL	LANE POSITION	ORDER OF FINISH	TIME

Fig. 16.12.   Sample Meet Card for Relay Races

throw, the second throw need not be marked. If there is a question, place a marker for each throw.

Remove markers after measuring preliminary throws. All height and distance measurements should be made with a steel tape graduated in quarter-inches.

BIBLIOGRAPHY

1. Amateur Athletic Union. *The A.A.U. Track and Field Handbook and Rules.* New York: The Amateur Athletic Union of the United States.
2. American Association for Health, Physical Education and Recreation. Division of Girls' and Women's Sport. *Track and Field Guide.* Washington, D.C., 1972–1974.
3. Breshnahan, George T., Tuttle, W. W., and Cretzmeyer, Francis X. *Track and Field Athletics.* St. Louis: C. V. Mosby, 1969.
4. Canahm, Don. *Track and Field Instructor's Guide.* Chicago: Athletic Institute, 1960.
5. Cratty, Bryant J. *Movement Behavior and Motor Learning.* Philadelphia: Lea and Febiger, 1964.
6. _____. "A Three Level Theory of Perceptual Motor Behavior," *Quest VI* (May 1966), 3–10.
7. Doberty, J. Kenneth. *Modern Track and Field* (2nd ed.). Englewood Cliffs, N.J.: Prentice-Hall, 1963, page 37.
8. _____. *Training for Running.* Englewood Cliffs, N. J.: Prentice-Hall, 1964.
9. Dyson, Geoffrey, H. G. *The Mechanics of Athletics* (4th ed.). London: University of London Press Ltd., 1967.
10. Foreman, Kenneth Everett, and Husted, Virginia. *Track and Field Techniques for Girls and Women* (2nd ed.). Dubuque, Iowa: W. C. Brown, 1971.
11. _____. *Track and Field.* Dubuque, Iowa: W. C. Brown, 1965.
12. Gustuson, Donald. "Weight Training Program for Women Participating in Track and Field," Paper presented to Women Coaches in Hawaii at a DGWS Workshop in Hawaii, 1964.
13. Henry, Franklin M. "Force—Time Characteristics of the Sprint Start," *The Research Quarterly,* October 1952, **23**, 3, 301–318.
14. International Amateur Athletic Federation. *Scoring Table for Women's Track and Field Events.* London: Council of the International Amateur Athletic Federation, 1954 (available through Track and Field News, Box 296, Los Altos, Calif. 94022).

15. Jackson, Nell C. *Track and Field for Girls and Women.* Minneapolis: Burgess, 1968.
16. Jokl, Ernst. "The Acquisition of Skill," *Quest VI* (May 1966), 11–15.
17. Jones, Tom. *How to Build a Track.* Los Altos, Calif.: Track and Field News (distributor), P.O. Box 296, 1955.
18. Jordon, Payton. "An Experimental Isometric Program for Track" (unpublished). Material sent to author from Payton Jordon, Head Track and Field Coach at Stanford University.
19. Jordon, Payton, and Spencer, Bud. *Champions in the Making.* Englewood Cliffs, N.J.: Prentice-Hall, 1969.
20. Kring, Roy F. *Complete Guide to High School Track and Field Coaching.* West Nyack, N.Y.: Parker Publishing Company, 1968.
21. Lane, Elizabeth, Obrecht, Donna, and Wienke, Phoebe (Consultants). *How to Improve Your Track and Field for Elementary School Children and Junior High School Girls.* Chicago: Athletic Institute.
22. Leighton, Jack R. *Progressive Weight Training.* New York: Ronald, 1961.
23. Miller, Kenneth Dayton. *Track and Field for Girls.* New York: Ronald, 1964.
24. National Collegiate Association. *The Official Collegiate Track and Field Guide.* Phoenix: College Athletics Publishing Service.
25. Parker, Virginia. *Track and Field for Girls and Women.* Philadelphia: W. B. Saunders, 1969.
26. Pearson, G. F. D. (Ed.) *Athletics.* New York: Thomas Nelson and Sons, 1964.
27. Quercetani, Roberto L. *A World History of Track and Field: 1864–1964.* New York: Oxford University Press, 1964.
28. Scott, Phebe M., and Crafts, V. R. *Track and Field for Girls and Women.* New York: Appleton-Century-Crofts, 1964.
29. Sealy, Victor C. *The Technique of Judging Track Events.* London: Amateur Athletic Association, 1967.
30. Thompson, Donnis H. *Women's Track and Field.* Boston: Allyn and Bacon, 1969.
31. *Track and Field News.* "Track and Field Market Place." P.O. Box 296, Los Altos, Calif. (Spring 1972).
32. Wakefield, Francis, Harkins, D., and Cooper, J. M. *Track and Field Fundamentals for Girls and Women.* St. Louis: C. V. Mosby (revised 1970).
33. *Women's Track and Field World.* $4.00 per year. P.O. Box 371, Claremont, Calif. 91711.

APPENDICES

APPENDIX A

EQUIPMENT AND SUPPLY COMPANIES

GENERAL EQUIPMENT AND SUPPLIES

The Harry Gill Company. P.O. Box 428, Urbana, Ill. (manufactures official implements and equipment)

J. Ridell, Inc. 2720 S. Des Plaines Ave., Des Plaines, Ill.

Wilson. 6141 Sheila St., Los Angeles, Calif.

Wolverine Sports, 745 State Circle, Ann Arbor, Mich.

SPECIALIZED EQUIPMENT AND SUPPLIES

Awards

The Program Aids Company, Inc. 550 Garden Ave., Mount Vernon, N.Y.

Body Weights

Elmer's Weights. P.O. Box 5426, Lubbock, Texas

Hurdles (breakaway type)

Leflar Athletic and Gym Equipment. 6840 S.W. Macadam Ave., Portland, Ore.

Javelins (aluminum)

"Dick Held" Javelins. P.O. Box 455, Lakeside, Calif.

Landing Pits

Thermo-Flex Inc. P.O. Box 1184, Salina, Kans. (manufactures "Cloud Nine" landing pits)

Markers (track curb markers)

Motivation Research Associates. 1351 Ruth Ave., St. Louis, Mo. 63122

Shoes

Adidas

U. S. distributors: Carlsen Import Shoe Company. 76 Franklin, New York, N.Y.

Vandernoot's Hardware. 213 Washington, Lansing, Mich.

Clifford Severn Sporting Goods. 10636 Magnolia Blvd., No. Hollywood, Calif.

H. B. Hughes Co. 2659 Fondren Dr., Dallas, Texas

Other Dealers

Blue Ribbon Sports. 3107 Pico Blvd., Suite A, Santa Monica, Calif.

Brooks Kangaroo Track Shoes. Brooks Athletic Shoes, Hanover, Pa.

Magnus Athletic Footwear. J. B. Athletic Shoe Company, Elizabethtown, Pa.

Puma Shoes, Sports Beconta, Inc. 440 Park Ave. South, New York, N.Y., or 91 Parklane, Brisbane, Calif.

Starting Blocks

Arnett Starting Block Company. P.O. Box 368, Harbor City, Calif.

Timing Devices (automatic performance analyzer)

Dekan Timing Devices. P.O. Box 712, Glen Ellyn, Ill.

APPENDIX B

FILMS, AUDIOVISUAL AIDS

FILMSTRIPS AND FILM LOOPS

1968 Champions. Women's loops. Relay, eight hundred and eighty meters. Hurdles, long jump, shot put, javelin, discus. Track and Field News. Box 296, Los Altos, Calif.

Women's Series 16mm. Women's loops, b & w. Set of slow-motion films featuring famous women athletes; covering sprint start, sprinting, hurdles, high jump, discus, shot put, long jump, running. Olympic Sportshelf. P.O. Box 634, New Rochelle, N.Y.

1960 Women's Olympic Loops. 16mm. loops, $1.75 ea.; 8mm. loops, $1.45 ea. Loops not in cartridges. Complete listings available upon request from the address below: include quality loops of top-ranking men and women athletes; loops taken during Olympics, Olympic trials, national, and international meets. Response to requests for information and orders is prompt when using air mail. Gary Butler. Little Hadham, Hertfordshire, England

Women's Track and Field. Super 8mm. loop, color ($18.95 per set, $144 complete). Outstanding sports technique loops featuring national champions and U.S. Olympic team members. Athletic Institute. 805 Merchandise Mart, Chicago, Ill.

FILMS

Fundamentals of Track and Field for Girls. Color, sound, Part I—*Track Events.* 16mm., 14 min., $152.50. Part II—*Field Events.* 16mm., 22 min., $220. Rental: $25 plus mailing. Specifically designed as teaching tools; emphasize form and technique. Designed to stimulate the girls' interest. Each event is presented in overall performance, with general principles broken down and analyzed, highlighted at key points. Association Film Services. 3419 W. Magnolia Blvd., Burbank, Calif.

Girls' Track Clinic. 16mm., b & w, sound, 14 min. Emphasizes organizational aspects of track. Shows guidance of high school beginners in practice and in meet participation. U.S. Olympic Headquarters. 57 Park Ave., New York, N.Y.

Olympic Films. 16mm., rental and sales. Payment with order or official school or institution purchase order required. 1960, 1964, 1968 instructional films are for *sale—prices* on request. 1954, 1956, 1960, 1964. Instructional and entertaining. Track and Field News. P.O. Box 296, Los Altos, Calif.

1968 Olympic Instructional. 16mm., b & w, full-length, 75 min. Rental: $25 per day; $50 per week. Slow motion studies of place winners in all field events and most running events. Women's Track and Field World. P.O. Box 371, Claremont, Calif.

1968 Olympic Instructional Film. 16mm. and 8mm., b & w, silent, 20 min. Rental: 16mm., $15 per day; 8mm., $10 per day; super 8mm., $20 per day. 400m. relay, 800m., 80m. hurdles, long jump, shot put, javelin. Track and Field News. P.O. Box 296, Los Altos, Calif.

Six Steps to the World Record (1967). 10 min., b & w, sound, $90, sale; $10, rental. A tribute to Vera Nikolic, the Yugoslav record holder and European champion of the 800m. McGraw-Hill Films, a Div. of McGraw-Hill Book Co. 327 W. 41st St., New York, N.Y. 10036

Tokyo Olympiad. Color, sound, $50, rental. A Jack Douglass presentation of the XVIII Olympic Games. The film depicts the revival of the Olympics after 1500 years of neglect. Idea Pictures. 34 Mac-Questen Parkway South, Mount Vernon, N.Y.

Track and Field for Elementary School Children and Junior High Girls. Color, sound, $18; color, silent, $15.25. Dashes, hurdles, relays, baton passing, long jump, high jump, ball throw, shot put. Athletic Institute, 805 Merchandise Mart, Chicago, Ill.

Track and Field for Girls and Women. Rental: $15 per day. Running and relays, jumping and weight events. Made in cooperation with AAU and Dr. Richard W. Willings. Teaching Aids Service. Visual Education Center, Floral Park, N.Y.

APPENDIX C

ENGLISH EQUIVALENTS OF METRIC DISTANCES

Meters	Miles	Yards	Feet	Inches
80		87	1	6
100		109	1	1
110		120	0	9
200		218	2	2
400		437	1	4
800		874	2	8
1,500		1,640	1	4
3,000	1	1,520	2	8
5,000	3	188	0	7
10,000	6	376	1	2
50,000	31	121	2	10

Approximate Timing Equivalents

The difference between 100 yards and 100 meters is about 9/10 second.

The difference between 220 yards and 200 meters is about 1/10 second.

The difference between 440 yards and 400 meters is about 3/10 second.

The difference between 880 yards and 800 meters is about 6/10 second.

The difference between 1 mile and 1,500 meters is about 17–18 seconds.

The difference between 3 miles and 5,000 meters is about 30 seconds.

The difference between 6 miles and 10,000 meters is about 60–65 seconds.

APPENDIX D

POINT SCORES FOR TRACK AND FIELD PERFORMANCES

Point Score	High Jump	Long Jump	Shot Put	100 Yd.	880 Yd.
50	4'6"	15'2"	27'2"	12.1	2:36.0
49		15'0"	26'9"		2:36.8
48	4'5"	14'10"	26'4"	12.2	2:37.6
47		14'8"	25'11"		2:38.4
46	4'4"	14'6"	25'6"	12.3	2:39.2
45		14'4"	25'1"		2:40.0
44	4'3"	14'2"	24'8"	12.4	2:40.8
43		14'0"	24'3"		2:41.6
42	4'2"	13'10"	23'10"	12.5	2:42.4
41		13'8"	23'5"		2:43.2
40	4'1"	13'6"	23'0"	12.6	2:44.0
39		13'4"	22'7"		2:44.8
38	4'0"	13'2"	22'2"	12.7	2:45.6
37		13'0"	21'9"		2:46.4
36	3'11"	12'10"	21'4"	12.8	2:47.2
35		12'8"	20'11"		2:48.0
34	3'10"	12'6"	20'6"	12.9	2:48.8
33		12'4"	20'1"		2:49.6
32	3'9"	12'2"	19'8"	13.0	2:50.4
31		12'0"	19'3"		2:51.2
30	3'8"	11'10"	18'10"	13.1	2:52.0
29		11'8"	18'5"	13.2	2:52.8
28	3'7"	11'6"	18'0"	13.3	2:53.6
27		11'4"	17'7"	13.4	2:54.4

Point Score	High Jump	Long Jump	Shot Put	100 Yd.	880 Yd.
26	3'6"	11'2"	17'2"	13.5	2:55.2
25		11'0"	16'9"	13.6	2:56.0
24	3'5"	10'10"	16'4"	13.7	2:57.0
23		10'8"	15'11"	13.8	2:58.0
22	3'4"	10'6"	15'6"	13.9	2:59.0
21		10'4"	15'1"	14.0	3:00.0
20	3'3"	10'2"	14'8"	14.1	3:02.0
19		10'0"	14'3"	14.2	3:04.0
18	3'2"	9'10"	13'10"	14.3	3:06.0
17		9'8"	13'5"	14.4	3:08.0
16	3'1"	9'6"	13'0"	14.5	3:10.0
15		9'4"	12'8"	14.6	3:13.0
14	3'0"	9'2"	12'4"	14.7	3:16.0
13		9'0"	12'0"	14.8	3:19.0
12	2'11"	8'10"	11'9"	14.9	3:22.0
11	2'10"	8'8"	11'6"	15.0	3:25.0
10	2'9"	8'6"	11'3"	15.2	3:28.0
9	2'8"	8'4"	11'0"	15.4	3:31.0
8	2'7"	8'2"	10'10"	15.6	3:34.0
7	2'6"	8'0"	10'8"	15.8	3:37.0
6	2'5"	7'10"	10'6"	16.0	3:40.0
5	2'4"	7'8"	10'4"	16.2	3:44.0
4	2'3"	7'6"	10'3"	16.4	3:48.0
3	2'2"	7'4"	10'2"	16.6	3:52.0
2	2'1"	7'2"	10'1"	16.8	3:56.0
1	2'0"	7'0"	10'0"	17.0	4:00.0
100	6'2"	23'6"	48'0"	9.8	1:56.0
99		23'4"	47'7"		1:56.8
98		23'2"	47'2"		1:57.6
97		23'0"	46'9"	9.9	1:58.4
96	6'1"	22'10"	46'4"		1:59.2
95		22'8"	45'11"		2:00.0
94		22'6"	45'6"	10.0	2:00.8
93		22'4"	45'1"		2:01.6
92	6'0"	22'2"	44'8"		2:02.4
91		22'0"	44'3"	10.1	2:03.2
90		21'10"	43'10"		2:04.0
89	5'11"	21'8"	43'5"		2:04.8
88		21'6"	43'0"	10.2	2:05.6
87		21'4"	42'7"		2:06.4
86	5'10"	21'2"	42'2"	10.3	2:07.2
85		21'0"	41'9"		2:08.0
84		20'10"	41'4"	10.4	2:08.8
83	5'9"	20'8"	40'11"		2:09.6
82		20'6"	40'6"	10.5	2:10.4
81		20'4"	40'1"		2:11.2
80	5'8"	20'2"	39'8"	10.6	2:12.0
79		20'0"	39'3"		2:12.8
78		19'10"	38'10"	10.7	2:13.6
77	5'7"	19'8"	38'5"		2:14.4
76		19'6"	38'0"	10.8	2:15.2

Point Score	High Jump	Long Jump	Shot Put	100 Yd.	880 Yd.
75		19'4"	37'7"		2:16.0
74	5'6"	19'2"	37'2"	10.9	2:16.8
73		19'0"	36'9"		2:17.6
72	5'5"	18'10"	36'4"	11.0	2:18.4
71		18'8"	35'11"		2:19.2
70	5'4"	18'6"	35'6"	11.1	2:20.0
69		18'4"	35'1"		2:20.8
68	5'3"	18'2"	34'8"	11.2	2:21.6
67		18'0"	34'3"		2:22.4
66	5'2"	17'10"	33'10"	11.3	2:23.2
65		17'8"	33'7"		2:24.0
64	5'1"	17'6"	33'5"	11.4	2:24.8
63		17'4"	33'0"		2:25.6
62	5'0"	17'2"	32'2"	11.5	2:26.4
61		17'0"	31'9"		2:27.2
60	4'11"	16'10"	31'4"	11.6	2:28.0
59		16'8"	30'11"		2:28.8
58	4'10"	16'6"	30'6"	11.7	2:29.6
57		16'4"	30'1"		2:30.4
56	4'9"	16'2"	29'8"	11.8	2:31.2
55		16'0"	29'3"		2:32.0
54	4'8"	15'10"	28'10"	11.9	2:32.8
53		15'8"	28'5"		2:33.6
52	4'7"	15'6"	28'0"	12.0	2:34.6
51		15'4"	27'7"		2:33.2

APPENDIX E

WEIGHT TRAINING EXERCISES

E.1.   Military Press. Clean weight to shoulders, using overhead grip. Using arms and shoulders, push weight overhead.

E.2. **Bench Press.** Lying supine on bench, take weight from buddy using overhead grip. Lower weight to chest, and push back to arms length.

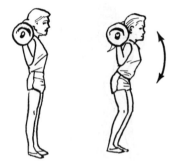

E.3. **One-Half Squat.** Take weight from rack, and squat to one-half squat.

E.4. **Sit-Ups.** Right elbow to left knee, left elbow to right knee. If more resistance is desired, elevate board. Lace fingers behind neck.

E.5. **Leg Curl and Raise.** Use iron boot. Lower, then bend forward and raise leg high to rear.

E.6. **One-Quarter to One-Half Squat.** One leg in contact with ground. Weight on shoulders. Execute squat, using lead leg for balance only.

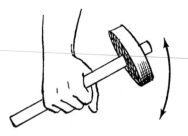

E.7. **Wrist Curl with Thumb-Up.** Use dumbbell loaded with 5-pound weight on one end only.

E.8. Leg Raise with Iron Boot. Use boot or sandbag. Raise leg forward with trunk coming down. Extend arms.

E.9. Leg Raise to Side Over Hurdle. Use iron boot or sandbag. Always go over forward.

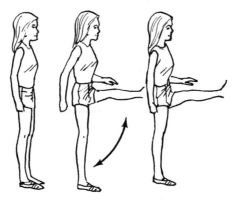

E.10. High Kick Using Iron Boot or Sandbag. Kick as in takeoff, using iron boot on lead foot. At the same time, raise on toe of takeoff foot.

E.11. Trunk Twister. Using wall weights, the back is to the weights. Pull weights forward, using trunk twisting motion. Keep arm straight.

E.12. Standing Triceps Pullover. Use dumbbell, 10 pounds, 15 repetitions. Keep elbow in same position as when weight is held overhead. Lower to behind neck, and elevate again.

WEIGHT TRAINING SCHEDULE

R — repetitions
S — sets
W — weight or pounds
BW — body weight

Exercise	Sprints	Middle Distance	Hurdles	Long Jump	High Jump	Discus	Shot Put	Javelin	General
Sit-ups	R-10 S-3 W-5	R-15 S-3 W-0	R-10 S-3 W-0	R-10 S-3 W-0	R-10 S-3 W-0	R-5 S-4 W-5	R-5 S-4 W-5	R-5 S-4 W-5	R-10 S-4 W-5
Leg Press Supine	R-10 S-2 W-½BW	R-15 S-2 W-¼BW	R-12 S-2 W-½BW	R-7 S-3 W-½BW	R-7 S-3 W-½BW	R-5 S-2 W-½BW	R-5 S-3 W-BW	R-5 S-2 W-¼BW	R-10 R-1 W-¼BW
Leg Curl	R-10 S-1 W-5	R-15 S-1 W-5	R-12 S-1 W-5	R-7 S-2 W-10	R-7 S-2 W-10	R-5 S-1 W-10	R-5 S-3 W-10	R-5 S-1 W-5	R-10 S-1 W-5
Leg Raise	R-10 S-1 W-10	R-15 S-1 W-5	R-12 S-2 W-5	R-7 S-2 W-10	R-7 S-3 W-10	R-5 S-1 W-15	R-5 S-2 W-20	R-5 S-1 W-10	R-10 S-1 W-5
Toe Raise	R-10 S-3 W-BW	R-15 S-2 W-½BW	R-10 S-3 W-BW	R-10 S-3 W-BW	R-10 S-3 W-BW	R-5 S-4 W-BW	R-5 S-4 W-BW	R-7 S-3 W-BW	R-10 S-1 W-¼BW
Half-Squat	R-10 S-3 W-½BW	R-15 S-2 W-¼BW	R-10 S-3 W-½BW	R-10 S-3 W-½BW	R-10 S-3 W-½BW	R-5 S-4 W-½BW	R-5 S-4 W-BW	R-7 S-3 W-½BW	R-10 S-1 W-¼BW
Stair Climb	R-20 steps W-30 S-3	R-40 W-20 S-2	R-20 steps W-30 S-3	R-20 W-30 S-3	R-10 W-30 S-3	R-10 W-30 S-4	R-10 steps W-40 S-4	R-20 steps W-30 S-3	R-20 steps W-10 S-1
Triplex Pulleys	R-10 S-1 W-light	R-15 S-1 W-light	R-10 S-1 W-light	R-5 S-3 W-heavy		R-5 S-3 W-heavy	R-5 S-3 W-heavy	R-5 S-3 W-heavy	R-10 S-1 W-light

Exercise	Sprints	Middle Distance	Hurdles	Long Jump	High Jump	Discus	Shot Put	Javelin	General
Bench Press						R-5 S-3 W	R-5 S-3 (limit of power for 3 sets)	R-5 S-3	R-7 S-2 W-½BW
Straddle Hops	R-15 S-1 W-40	R-20 S-1 W-25	R-15 S-2 W-40	R-10 S-3 W-50	R-10 S-3 W-50	R-5 S-2 W-60	R-5 S-3 W-60	R-10 S-2 W-40	R-25 S-1 W-20
Calf Flexors	W	(boot should provide enough resistance to tire muscle in regular R's)		R-10 S-2	R-10 S-2		R-10 S-2		R-10 S-1
Leg Extension		(iron) (boots)	R-10 S-1 W-5	R-10 S-1 W-5	R-10 S-1 W-5				R-10 S-1 W-5
Sprint	50 yd. W-20 S-3		50 yd. W-20 S-3						50 yd. S-1 W-10
Half-Speed Run		220 yd. W-10							220 yd. W-10 S-1
One-Leg Squat			(start with one and increase till difficulty prevents further R's)			use 10 or 20 lb. if possible			3 one-leg squats excellent
Half-Squat Jump				R-5 S-1 W-10	R-5 S-1 W-10				R-5 S-1 W-10
Trampoline or Springboard				about 3—5 min. periods					one 5-min. period

APPENDIX G

ISOMETRIC EXERCISES

Note that the muscle group exercises precede the isometric exercises.

G.1.   Gastrocnemius Press. Stand on toes and press upward against partner's hands.

G.2.   Biceps Femoral Pull. Hold arms at elbow level, elbows bent. Push forward, palms up.

G.3.   Pectoralis Press. Push with hands clasped in front of chest, elbows up and out.

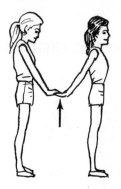

G.4. Triceps Pull. Exert pressure in back of body, arms straight and palms up.

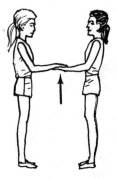

G.5. Latissimus Press. With arms bent at elbows, press upward, palms up.

G.6. Deltoid Press. Hold arms out at shoulder level. Press upward against partner's hands and arms. Palms down.

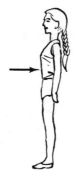

G.7. Abdominal Press. In standing position, attempt to bring the navel to the spine.

APPENDIX H

CALISTHENIC EXERCISES

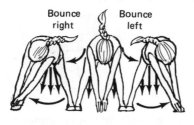

H.1. Trunk Twisting—Legs Apart.

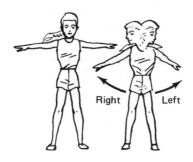

H.2. Body Rotation from "Up" Position.

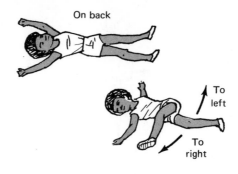

H.3. Cross Leg Hip Rotation.

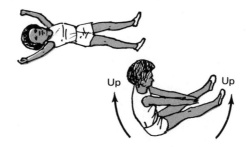

H.4. Jackknife Sit-Ups for Stomach.

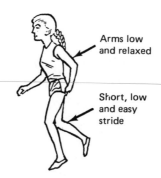

H.5. Light Jogging. Use a short, easy stride and low arm action to avoid tension.

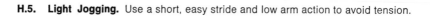

H.6.   Trunk Twister and Alternate Toe Touching.

H.7.   Push-Ups. Do these from flat hand and fingertips.

H.8.   Inverted Bicycle Pedal, with Leg Kick.

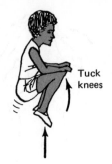

H.9.   Knee Lifts. Jump into air, and bring knees to chest.

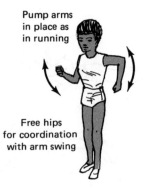

H.10.   Pumping Arms. Relax and coordinate hips.

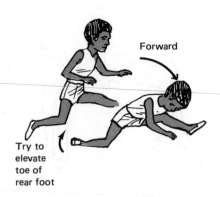

H.11.   Hurdle Exercise. Rotate upper body completely around hips from this position.

Right   Left

H.12. Alternate Leg Touch. Do this from sitting position.

H.13. Reaction Running. Run in place against firm pole or wall.

Lean
forward

Raise
on toe

H.14. Leg Stretcher.

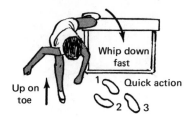

H.15. Back Leg Snap. Snap leg with three quick steps off hurdle.

H.16. Crotch-Hip Stretch. Stretch to right and left.

H.17. Trunk Swinging. Swing to right and left.

H.18.   High Leg Kick.

H.19.   Medicine Ball Throw. Throw from shot-put position high overhead into backboard.

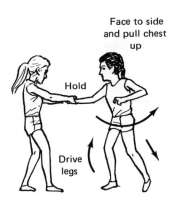

H.20.   Pairs for Discus Throwing.

H.21.   Jump Pike. This is often done into sawdust from a run and jump over crossbar.

H.22.   Bounding. Bound from right and left feet while trotting.

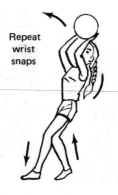

H.23.   Medicine Ball Wrist Snap. Repeat into backboard or wall for shot put.

H.24. Javelin Back Flexibility. Exercise in pairs.

H.25. Javelin Side Strength. Exercise in pairs.

H.26. Javelin Back Strength. Back arcs.

APPENDIX I

ANNUAL TRAINING SCHEDULES

The following training schedules are primarily for the coach and athlete who are seeking very sophisticated results and intend to strive toward excellence. These schedules are not for the typical student in a physical education class, simply because such a person does not have the physical preparedness for the ardor involved. Therefore, it is strongly recommended that the teacher or student in the school class situation use the learning exercises or drills included in the description of each event, plus review sequences of experiences specifically included in the teaching unit.

The training schedule is based upon an eleven-month period. Although many competitive programs only run for half that period— i.e., January to June, or April to August—there must be some effort to avoid an inactive period of seven months if excellence and reaching a maximum potential is of concern. The athlete must keep very active even if it involves playing soccer, basketball, volleyball, or following this schedule individually without other members of the track team. It is almost an impossible task for a coach to get an athlete who is totally out of condition in top shape by the big meet five months hence. However, for the track season, which is to run for five months, this training schedule can be followed with these adjustments:

preparatory period runs for two months

precompetitive period, for one and one-half months

competitive period, remainder of season

As one reads this section, it is clear that the training schedule has been briefly stated. All terms appearing in the workout schedules have been fully explained in Chapter 13, which is related to general training techniques. The terms used and the progressive changes suggested in each phase will be better understood if that section is reviewed.

There are inconsistencies in the professional research related to warm-ups The degree to which warm-up prevents injuries or facilitates performance has been challenged. For these reasons, the author feels it necessary to qualify these suggested exercises. At this point, it is difficult for her to ignore an attempt to denote as meaningless sequential movements which lead to the program to be followed for a specific workout. To move from the locker room into taking starts or throwing a javelin seems a great disservice to the body, although more recent research does not agree with this statement. For the sake of communication, this section is referred to as warm-ups; it is probably closer allied with additional conditioning. It is an opportunity to run additional amounts, plus a provision to perform stretching and limbering exercises.

A daily warm-up should take a minimum of 20 minutes:

jogging

exercises

wind sprints

warm up to the skills or activity of the day*

Points one-four listed below are parts of the total warm-up:

1. Jogging laps.
2. Exercises—full description listed in Appendix H.
3. Wind sprints—60 yards:
   1 or 2 times at ¼ speed
   1 or 2 times at ½ speed
   2 or 3 times at ¾ speed
   1 or 2 times at full speed
4. Five minutes rest while changing into spikes or going to one's event for the day's practice schedule.

A warm-down, consisting of jogging at least two laps or a half-mile, is as important as the warm-up.

SPRINTER'S WORKOUT SHEET†

A   Warm-up: Jog ½ mile, calisthenics, six wind sprints (¼, ½, ¾ speed)

---

*For example, throwing events might include gradual movements into the event—putting from a stand, finger flips, throwing javelin into the ground, etc. A warm-up for starting would comprise several light starts.

†For an understanding of applying this sheet to a daily schedule, please refer to the table on page 244.

B	*Fartlek:* Speedplay 5 miles—hills, even terrain, and grassy area
C	*Fartlek:* 2–3 miles—uphill and downhill running, 70 yards each. Bounding forward.
D	Wind sprints on grass: work on form—foreleg reach, high knee action, curve running
E	220 at ¾ effort: Concentrate on relaxation
F	110: Competition speed (from blocks)
G	660: Run distance between 1:50 and 2:10 (10-minutes rest in-between)
H	440: ¾ effort (3-minutes rest in-between)
I	440: 58–63 seconds (6-minutes rest in-between)
J	330: 9/10 speed (5–7 minutes rest in-between)
K	220: Competition speed
L	220: ¾ effort—concentrate on relaxation
M	150: 9/10 effort from starting block (1½-minutes rest between each)
N	150: Competition speed from blocks (4-minutes rest in-between)
O	80: From the blocks (1½-minutes rest)
P	60: Full speed work on lean at finish line
Q	50: Full speed from starting blocks
R	Time-trials
S	Competition
T	Relay
U	Warm-down: Jog 2 laps
V	Starts: 3 out 20 yards; 3–5 out 30 yards
W	Weight program
X	Isometric exercises
Y	Curve running: Run into curve, posture on curve, posture coming off
Z	Straightaway intervals: Run straightaways, walk curves

SPRINTER'S SCHEDULE*

	Mon.	Tue.	Wed.	Thur.	Fri.	Sat.	Sun.
Preparatory Season—October through February							
October– November	W A	A D6	X G2	A H3	 W		

*Letters correspond to distances to be run or tasks to be performed listed on the corresponding Workout Sheet. Numbers denote the number of times the task is to be performed.

	C	Z6	D6	O4	A C
	U	U	U	U	U
December– January	A	W	A	W	A
	G2	J3	G2	H3	J3
	D6	P4	D6	P4	D6
	U	U	U	U	U
February	X	A V8	X A	A	A
	A	M4	J3	V10	X
	H3	O4		M4 O4	J3 T
	P4 U	U	U	U	U

Precompetitive Season—March through May

March	AX	A	AX	A	AX
	K5	V8	K2	V8	L3
		M2 O2	Q3	P8	T
	U	U	U	U	U
April	X AD	AD	AD X	AD	X AD
	K5	P5	O5	V8	R
	T U	M2 U	T U	O2 U	U
May	AD	X AD	AD	X AD	AD
	V6	K2	N2	J2	R
	F6	T	V4	T P6	T
	U	U	U	U	U

Competitive Season—June through August

June	AD	AD	AD	AD	AD
	K3	V15	O4	V10	S
	D6	T	M1	P6	T
	U	U	U	U	U

July†	ATU	AF5 U8 U	ATU	rest U	S
August‡	A J2	A V15 T	A Y	rest	S

QUARTER-MILER'S WORKOUT SHEET*

A	30-min. warm-up: Jog ¾ mile, exercises, wind sprints; competition warm-up
B	*Fartlek:* 5 miles
C	*Fartlek:* 2–3 miles
D	Wind sprints on grass: 70 yards each; work on form, foreleg reach, high knee action, curve running
E	Rest
F	110 yd.: 10-min. rest between full speed (from blocks)
G	660: Run distance 1:38 to 1:48
H	550: 20 seconds slower than 440 competition time
I	440: 58 to 69 seconds ⅞ effort (5-min. rest)
J	440: 69 to 72 seconds ¾ effort (3-min. rest)
K	330: Full speed; relaxed (10-min. rest in-between)
L	220: Competition speed
M	220: 8/10 effort (1½-min. rest in-between)
N	150: Full speed from blocks (3-min. rest in-between)
O	150: 16–19 sec.
P	80: Full speed from blocks (5-min. rest in-between)
Q	100: 13 sec. and 3 min. 300 yards recovery laps
R	Time-trials
S	Competition
T	Relay
U	Warm-down: Jog 2 laps
V	Starts: Out to 35 yards
W	Weight room
X	Isometric exercises
Y	Curve running: Run into curve, posture on curve, posture coming off
Z	Straightaway intervals: Run straightaways, walk curves

†The program fluctuates from week to week during July and August. Schedules should be prepared on a weekly basis, depending on individual needs indicated in competition.

‡Emphasize speed and perfection of technique while maintaining the high level of physical conditioning thus far obtained.

*For an understanding of applying this sheet to a daily schedule, please refer to the table on the next page.

QUARTER-MILER'S SCHEDULE*

	Mon.	Tue.	Wed.	Thur.	Fri.	Sat.	Sun.
Preparatory Season—October through February							
October– November	A C	A C	A C	A C	A C	A C	
	W	X	W	X	W	W	
	U	U	U	U	U	U	
December–	B	A	B	A	B		
January	X	W	X	W	X		
		K4		K4		C	
		U		U			
February	A	A	A	A	A		
	G3	X	J6	X	M10	B	
	D6	M10	O6	C	T		
	U	U	U	U	U		
Precompetitive Season—March through May							
March	A	A	A	A	A		
	G3	M10	G3	J5	K4		
	V6	O2	V6	O5	V6	C	
	U	U	U	U	U		
April	AC	AX	A	A	A		
	W	M10	K4 W	X	R	C	
	U	U	U	N6 U	U		
May	A	A	X	A	A		
	X	J8	G1	P15	X		
	G3	V3	J4	V3	R		
	O2 U	U	U	U	U		

*Letters correspond to distances to be run or tasks to be performed listed on the corresponding Workout Sheet. Numbers denote the number of times the task is to be performed.

Competitive Season—June through August					
June	A	A	A	A.	
	H3	L4	K4	F6	E	S
	U	U	U	U		
July†	N	K	G	F	P	S
August‡						

HALF-MILER'S WORKOUT SHEET*

A   Warm-up: 1 to 1½ mile jog and exercises

B   *Fartlek:* Two workouts—A.M., 3–4 miles; P.M., 3–4 miles

C   *Fartlek:* 5 miles

D   *Fartlek:* 6 miles

E   *Fartlek:* 7 miles

F   *Fartlek:* Two workouts—A.M., easy run 4–5 miles; P.M., interval workout

G   ¾ of a mile to 3:45 to 3:25—10–15-min. rest in-between

H   880: 10-min. rest in-between

I   660: 1:47 to 1:38 sec., 10–15-min. rest in-between

J   440: Start at 7 sec., 4-min. rest; work down to 68 sec., 3-min. rest

K   440: Under 62 sec., 5–7-min. rest

L   220: Start at 36 sec., 2-min. rest; work down to 30 sec., 1-min. rest

M   220: under 29 sec., 5-min. rest

N   150: 9/10 effort

O   100: From starting blocks

P   330: 9/10 effort

Q   Run 330, jog 330; run 220, jog 220; run 110, jog 110; continue without stopping for ½ hour

R   Time-trials

S   Competition

T   Relay

U   Warm-down: Jog 2–4 laps

†The program fluctuates from week to week during July and August. Schedules should be prepared on a weekly basis, depending on individual needs indicated during competition. Closely approximate the sprinter's program plus a few days as with the half-miler.

‡Emphasize speed and perfection of technique while maintaining the high level of physical conditioning thus far obtained. Closely approximate with the sprinter's program.

*For an understanding of applying this sheet to a daily schedule, please refer to the table on the next page.

V   Starts: To 50-yard mark
W   Weight room
X   Isometric exercises
Y   Strategy: Pass coming off curve and just before going into curve
Z   Rest day

HALF-MILER'S SCHEDULE*

	Mon.	Tue.	Wed.	Thur.	Fri.	Sat.	Sun.
Preparatory Season—October through February							
October–November	W	X	W	X	W		
	B		B		B		B
		C		C		C	
December–January	A	A	A	A	A	A	A
	Q	D	B	D	B	D	C
	U		U		U		U
February	A	A	A	J6	A	A	
	H3		Q		D	M6	B
	N2	B		N3			
	U	U				U	
Precompetitive Season—March through May							
March		Q		H3		J10	
		B	N3	B		B	C
			U		U		
April	A	A	A	A	A		
	G3	J10	L10-15	H3	R	C	C
	U	U	U	U	U		

*Letters correspond to distances to be run or tasks to be performed listed on the corresponding Workout Sheet. Numbers denote the number of times the task is to be performed.

May	A	A	A	A	A		
	J10	L10-15	H3	C	R	C	C
	U	U	U	U	U		

Competitive Season—June through August

June	A	A	A	A		
	J10	L10	H3	L5	C	A
	U	U	U	U		S
July†				T			
	J10	L10	H3	I2	R	S	C
August‡	C	J5	L5	I2	R	S	
		N3	O4	P1			

MIDDLE-DISTANCE AND DISTANCE PACE CHART*

220 Yards	One-Quarter Mile	One-Half Mile	Three-Quarter Mile	One Mile
0:39	0:78	2:42	4:06	5:30
0:38	0:76	2:37	3:58	5:20
0:37	0:74	2:33	3:52	5:12
0:36	0:73	2:29	3:64	5:04
0:36	0:72	2:26	3:41	4:56
0:34	0:69	2:21	3:33	4:45
0:33	0:67	2:16	3:28	4:40
0:33	0:66	2:13	3:22	4:32
0:32	0:65	2:11	3:17	4:24
0:32	0:64	2:08	3:13	4:16
0:30	0:61	2:04	3:07	4:08

DISTANCE RUNNER'S WORKOUT SHEET†

A	Warm-up: Jog 1 mile exercise
B	Run a total of 40 miles per week in two workouts per day

†The program fluctuates from week to week during July and August. Schedules should be prepared on a weekly basis, depending on individual needs indicated during competition.

‡Emphasize speed and perfection of technique while maintaining the high level of physical conditioning thus far obtained.

*The figure to the left is the time in which that particular segment of the race could be run to reach the desired time for the total distance of the race.

†For an understanding of applying this sheet to a daily schedule, please refer to the table on the next page.

C	Run a total of 50 miles per week in two workouts per day
D	Run a total of 60 miles per week in two workouts per day
E	*Fartlek:* A.M., easy run 4–5 miles; P.M., interval workout
F	*Fartlek:* A.M., run 2 miles on sand; P.M., 3–5 miles
G	*Fartlek:* A.M., run hills; P.M., 5–7 miles
H	*Fartlek:* Easy, for ½ hour
I	*Fartlek:* Easy, for 20 min.
J	*Fartlek:* Easy, for 70 min.
K	¾ of a mile: 3:30 for one and 4:00 to 3:45
L	880: 2:40 to 2:20 (10-min. rest in-between)
M	660: 1:52 to 1:42 (10-min. rest in-between)
N	440: 80 to 69 (3-min. rest in-between) At beginning of season, start closer 80; at end of season, run closer to 70's.
O	440: 2 sec. off pace time (5–7-min. rest in-between)
P	220: 36 sec. to 28 sec.
Q	220: 9/10 effort
R	150: 9/10 speed
S	Run 330, jog 330; run 220, jog 220; run 110, jog 110; continue without stopping for 45 min.
T	Time-trials or competition
U	Relay
V	Warm-down: Jog 4 laps each 1 mile
W	*Fartlek:* Easy, 3 miles
X	*Fartlek:* Easy, 5 miles
Y	Strategy — Passing coming off curves and just before going into curve
Z	Rest day

DISTANCE RUNNER'S SCHEDULE*

	Mon.	Tue.	Wed.	Thur.	Fri.	Sat.	Sun.
Preparatory Season—October through February							
January–February	B	B	B	B	B	B	B

*Letters correspond to distances to be run or tasks to be performed listed on the corresponding Workout Sheet. Numbers denote the number of times the task is to be performed.

March–	C	C	C	C	C	C	C
April	C	C	C	C	C	C	C
May	A	A	A	A	A	A	A
	F		F		F		
		W		W		X	W
	U	U	U	U	U	U	U

Precompetitive Season—June through August

June	A	A	A	A	A		
	W	G1	O6	G		S	
	R4	R4	I		W		X
	U	U	U	U	U	U	
July	A	A	A		A		
	N10	L5	N10	J	T	J	H
	U	U	U		U		
August	A	A	A	A		A	
	N10	L5	K3	N10	J	T	H
	U	U	U	U		U	

Competitive Season—September through December

September						A	
	A	A	A				H
	N10	N10	L4	H	Z	R	
	U	U	U				
October†	A		T	Z			
	L6	N10	K	H	Z	T	H
November–December‡	H	N10	T	Z	Z	T	
			L1				

For the cross-country competitor a 12-month program is suggested, starting with Jan. and building up to a highly competitive season in the Fall. Therefore Oct. and Nov. schedule should be started in Jan. and follow through with the schedules for Aug. in Dec.

†The program fluctuates from week to week during October and November. Schedules should be prepared on a weekly basis, depending on individual needs indicated during competition.

‡Emphasize speed and perfection of technique while maintaining the high level of physical conditioning thus far obtained.

HURDLER'S WORKOUT SHEET*

A	Warm-up: Hurdle stretching exercises and hurdle drills
B	Speed over 8 hurdles
C	*Fartlek:* 2–3 miles (include uphill and downhill running)
D	Wind sprints on grass: 70 yards, bounding forward, fore-leg reach, high knee action
E	Run over 12 hurdles (speed run)
F	Starts over 1st and 2nd hurdles
G	660: Run distance between 1:50 and 2:10 (10–15-min. rest in-between)
H	Isometrics
I	440: ¾ effort (3-min. rest in-between)
J	330: 9/10 speed (5–7-min. rest in-between)
K	220: Competitions speed
L	220: ¾ effort; concentrate on relaxation
M	150: 9/10 effort from starting blocks (1½-min. rest between each)
N	Weight room
O	80: From the blocks (1½-min. rest in-between)
P	60: Full speed work on driving off last hurdle (past) the finish line
Q	Starts: Over first, second, third, and fourth hurdles
R	Time-trials
S	Competition
T	Relay
U	Warm-down: Jog 2 laps
V	Starts: Over first hurdle
W	Form over four hurdles (lead leg, trail leg)
X	Speed: Over 6 hurdles
Y	Complete flight
Z	Run straightaways, walk curves

HURDLER'S SCHEDULE†

	Mon.	Tue.	Wed.	Thur.	Fri.	Sat.	Sun.
Preparatory Season—October through February							
October–	N	A	H	AD	N		

*For an understanding of applying this sheet to a daily schedule, please refer to the table below and on the next page.

†Letters correspond to distances to be run or tasks to be performed listed on the corresponding Workout Sheet. Numbers denote the number of times the task is to be performed.

November	AD	D6	G2	I3	AD
	C6	Z6	D6	P4	C6
	U	U	U	U	U
December–	A	N	AH	N	A
January	G2	J3	W	I3	J3
	D6	P4	D6	P4	D6
	U	U	U	U	U
February	AH	A	AH	A	AH
	J2	V8	J2	V10	E2
	X4	W6	F5	X4	F5
	U	U	U	U	U

Precompetitive Season—March through May

March	ADH	AD	ADH	AD	ADH
	E3	B4	Q6	B4	K6
	Y3	T Q3	E3	Q3	T P3
	U	U	U	U	U
April	AD	AD	AD	AD	AD
	J2	V10	J2	F10	R3
	M	Y3	M	B4	T
May	T	LZ	T	W4	U
	AD	AD	AD	AD	AD
	J2	F10	J2	E3	R3
	O6	B4	O6	F6	T
		W4		L2	
	U	U	U	U	U

Competitive Season—June through August

June†				S	
				T	

†Emphasis is predominantly based upon perfecting movement and speed work, while maintaining excellent physical condition. The program fluctuates from week to week, and schedules are now made out weekly, based upon needs indicated during competition.

July‡	S
August§	T

LONG JUMPER'S WORKOUT SHEET*

A   Warm-up: Jog ½ mile, calisthenics, six wind sprints (¼, ½, ¾ speed)

B   *Fartlek:* 2–3 miles

C   Weight program

D   Wind sprints on grass: Use bouncing steps as in the long jump approach. Work on approach steps away from long jump area.

E   220 at ¾ effort: Concentrate on relaxation

F   Isometric exercises

G   660: Run distance between 1:50 and 2:10 (10-min. rest in-between)

H   Competition

I   440: 58–63 sec. (6-min. rest in-between)

J   330: 9/10 speed (5–7-min. rest in-between)

K   220: 9/10 to full speed

L   Warm-down: Jog two laps

M   150: 9/10 effort from blocks

N   Time-trials

O   80: From the blocks (1½-min. rest)

P   50: From the blocks

Q   Work on steps in the approach, and rest between each approach

R   Pop-ups: Use hurdle or string to practice jumping for height

S   Jump for distance and measure

T   Emphasize lifting action

U   Emphasize proper landing (extend legs)

V   Rest

W   Pop-ups

X   Arch and extend legs, if this technique is to be used

Y   Curve running: Posture into, on, and coming off curve

Z   Straightaway intervals: Run straightaways, walk curves

‡The program fluctuates from week to week during July and August. Schedules should be prepared on a weekly basis, depending on individual needs indicated during competition.

§Emphasize speed and perfection of technique while maintaining the high level of physical conditioning thus far obtained.

*For an understanding of applying this sheet to a daily schedule, please refer to the table on page 256.

LONG JUMPER'S SCHEDULE*

	Mon.	Tue.	Wed.	Thur.	Fri.	Sat.	Sun.
Preparatory Season—October through February							
October– November	C A	A	C A	A	C A		
	B	D6 Z10	D6	Z10	B	B	
	L	L	L	L	L		
December– January	A	CA	A	A C	A		
	G2	J3	G2	I3	J3	B	
	D6	P4	D6	P4	D6		
	L	L	L	L	L		
February	A F	A	A F	A	A F		
	V15	Q10 R10	V15	Q10 W10	J3	B	
	M4	K4	M4	J3	Y4		
	L	L	L	L	L		
Precompetitive Season—March through May							
March	A F	A	A F	A Q10	A F		
	D6	Q10 R10	D6	R10	D6	B	
	J2 O6	U5	M5 O6	U5 X	S3		
		X			K4		
	L	L	L	L	L		
April	AD6 F	AD6	AD6 F	AD6	AD6 F		
	J2	P6	O4	P6	S6		

*Letters correspond to distances to be run or tasks to be performed listed on the corresponding Workout Sheet. Numbers denote the number of times the task is to be performed.

	T	O4	Y6	O4	T	
	L	M2L	L	M2L	L	
May	A	A	A	A	A	
	Q10	F	Q10	F	Q10	
		J2		J2		
	R10	P9	R10	P9	R10	S6
	U5		U5		U5	
	X	T	X	T	X	TN
	L	L	L	L	L	

Competitive Season—June through August

		A	A	A	A	
June	A	F	Q10	F	Q10	
	Q10			J2		
	R10	J2	R10	P9	R10	
		P9	U5	P9	U5	
	U5	T	X	T	X	H
	X					
	L	L	L	L	L	
July†					H	
August‡					H	

HIGH JUMPER'S WORKOUT SHEET*

A	Warm-up: Jog ½ mile, calisthenics, six wind sprints (¼, ½, ¾ speed)
B	*Fartlek:* 2–3 miles
C	Weight room
D	Wind sprints on grass: Use bouncy steps similar to those used in high jump approach.
E	220 at ¾ effort: Concentrate on relaxation
F	Isometric exercises
G	660: Run distance between 1:50 and 2:10 (10-min. rest in-between)
H	Competition

†The program fluctuates from week to week during July and August. Schedules should be prepared on a weekly basis, depending on individual needs indicated during competition.

‡Emphasize speed and perfection of technique while maintaining the high level of physical conditioning thus far obtained.

*For an understanding of applying this sheet to a daily schedule, please refer to the table on page 258.

I	440: 58 to 67 (6-min. rest in-between)
J	330: 9/10 speed (5–7-min. rest in-between)
K	220: 9/10 to full speed
L	Warm-down: Jog 2 laps
M	150: 9/10 effort from blocks
N	Time-trials
O	80: From blocks
P	50: From blocks
Q	Work on steps in the approach, and rest between each approach
R	Bar at 4 feet 6 inches: Work on layout form
S	Start 8 inches below maximum height, jump, and raise bar 2 inches after each successful jump
T	Use 4 steps and jump
U	Emphasize roll at 4-foot height
V	Emphasize high kicks after spring
W	Put bar at 2 inches below maximum height; work on take-off and roll
X	Work on trampoline
Y	Curve running: Posture into, on, and coming off curve
Z	Straightaway intervals: Run straightaways, walk curves

HIGH JUMPER'S SCHEDULE*

	Mon.	Tue.	Wed.	Thur.	Fri.	Sat.	Sun.
Preparatory Season—October through February							
October– November	CX A	A D6	CX A	A	CX A		
	B L	Z10	D6	Z10	B	B	
		L	L	L	L		
December– January		CX					
	A	A	A	AC	A		
	G2	J3	G2	I3	J3	B	
	D6	P4	D6	P4	D6		
	L	L	L	L	L		
February	A		A		A		
	F	A	F	A	F		

*Letters correspond to distances to be run or tasks to be performed listed on the corresponding Workout Sheet. Numbers denote the number of times the task is to be performed.

V15	Q10 R10	V15	Q10 R10	J3	B
M4	K4	M4	K4	Y4	
L	L	L	L	L	

Precompetitive Season—March through May

Month						
March	A F	A	AF	A Q10	AF	
	D6	Q10 R10	D6	R10	D6	B
	J2 O6	U5	M5 O6	U5	S3	
		X		X	K4	
	L	L	L	L	L	
April	AD6	AD6	F AD6	AD6	AD6 F	
	F J2	P6	O4	P6	S	
	L	O4 M2L	Y6 L	O4 M2L	T L	
May	A Q10	AF	A Q10	AF	A Q10	A
	R10	J2	R10	J2	R10	S6
	U5 X	P9 T	U5 X	P9 T	U5 X	T N
	L	L	L	L	L	

Competitive Season—June through August

Month						
June	A	AF	A Q10	AF	A Q10	
	Q10 R10	J2	R10	J2	R10	
	U5	P9 T	U5 X	P9 T	U5 X	H
	L	L	L	L	L	
July†						H
August‡						H

†The program fluctuates from week to week during July and August. Schedules should be prepared on a weekly basis, depending on individual needs indicated during competition.

‡Emphasize speed and perfection of technique while maintaining the high level of physical conditioning thus far obtained.

SHOT-PUTTER'S WORKOUT SHEET*

A	Warm-up: Jog ½ mile, exercises, six wind sprints, finger flips
B	*Fartlek:* 1–2 miles
C	Weight room
D	Wind sprints on grass
E	220: ¾ effort; concentrate on relaxation
F	Isometric exercises
G	660: Run distance between 2:30 and 2:45 (15-min. rest in-between)
H	Competition
I	440: Easy
J	330: 7/8 to 9/10 effort (6-min. rest in-between)
K	220: 9/10 effort (5–7-min. rest in-between)
L	Warm-down: Jog 2 laps
M	80: From blocks
N	Starts: Out 35 yards
O	Glide across circle without shot
P	From a stand, put a 12-pound shot
Q	Total action across circle (include the reverse)
R	Official shot: Put from a stand
S	Total action across circle (exclude reverse)
T	Put: Measure and record
U	Emphasize extension and lift
V	Concentrate on specifics: Putting foot underneath as glide ends, hip rotation, left foot placement at board, remaining in closed position, arm movements
W	Rest
X	Relay work
Y	50 yards: Hard, using standing start
Z	Straightaway intervals: Run straightaways, walk curves

SHOT-PUTTER'S SCHEDULE†

	Mon.	Tue.	Wed.	Thur.	Fri.	Sat.	Sun.
Preparatory Season—October through February							
October–November	C	A F	C	A F	C		

*For an understanding of applying this sheet to a daily schedule, please refer to the table below and on page 261.

†Letters correspond to distances to be run or tasks to be performed listed on the corresponding Workout Sheet. Numbers denote the number of times the task is to be performed.

B	D8	B	D8	B
	L		L	
December–January A C	A F	A C	A F	A C
B	Z6	B	Z6	B
	O12		O12	
	L		L	
February A C	A F	A C	A F	A C
C1	P15	J2	P15	K3
O10	R4 S10	O10	R4 S10	O10
P12 L	D4 L	P12 L	D4 L	P12 L

Precompetitive Season—March through May

March A C	A F	A C	A F	A C
J2	P6	K2	P6	I2
Y6	Q15	N6	Q15	T6
L	U10 L	L	U10 L	D4 L
April A C	A F	A C	A F	A C
X	Y20	O20	V20	T6
L N6	L	L Z6	L	L N6
May AC	A F	AC	A F	AC
X	D6		D6	T6
R8 V20	V10	R8 V20	V10	
S8 L	L	Q8 L	L	L

Competitive Season—June through August

June AC	A F	AC	A F	AC

	X	P6	D6	R6 S8	D6	T
	O10 V10	S8 Q10	U10 V10	Q15		
	L	N6 L	Q2 L	N6 L		
July†	AC X	F D6	AC D6	F D6	AC DC	H
August‡	AF X	AF D6	AF D6	AF D6	AF D6	H

DISCUS THROWER'S WORKOUT SHEET*

A	Warm-up: Jog ½ mile, exercises, 6 wind sprints
B	*Fartlek:* 1–2 miles
C	Weight room: Medicine ball exercise (see Chapter 2)
D	Wind sprints on grass
E	220: at ¾ effort; concentrate on relaxation
F	Isometric exercises
G	660: Run distance between 2:30 and 2:45 (15-min. rest in-between)
H	Competition
I	440: Easy
J	330 at 7/8 to 9/10 effort (6-min. rest in-between)
K	220 at 9/10 effort (5–7-min. rest in-between)
L	Warm-down: Jog 2 laps
M	80: From starting blocks
N	Starts: Out to 35 yards
O	Glide across; work on one turn across circle
P	Throw from a stand: Use heavier discus
Q	Total action across circle: Tap discus to hand
R	Throw from a stand: Use official weight discus
S	Total action across circle: Throw, but minimize the reverse
T	Throw: Measure and record
U	Emphasize extension and lift

†The program fluctuates from week to week during July and August. Schedules should be prepared on a weekly basis, depending on individual needs indicated during competition.

‡Emphasize speed and perfection of technique while maintaining the high level of physical conditioning thus far obtained.

*For an understanding of applying this sheet to a daily schedule, please refer to the table on page 263.

V	Concentrate on closed body position when reaching the throwing stance, use hips, check delayed arm action, discus trajectory
W	Rest
X	Relay work
Y	50 yards (hard): Use standing start
Z	Straightaway intervals: Run straightaways, walk curves

DISCUS THROWER'S SCHEDULE*

	Mon.	Tue.	Wed.	Thur.	Fri.	Sat.	Sun.
Preparatory Season—October through February							
October–November	C	A F	C	A F	C		
	B	D8	B	D8	B		
		L		L			
December–January	A C	A F	A C	A F	A C		
	B	Z6	B	Z6	B		
		O12		O12			
		L		L			
February	A C	A F	A C	A F	A C		
	G1	P15 R4	J2	P15 R4	K3		
	O10	S10	O10	S10	O10		
	P12 L	D4 L	P12 L	D4 L	P12 L		
Precompetitive Season—March through May							
March	A C	A F	A C	A F	A C		
	J2	S20	K2	S20	I2		
	Y6	R20	N6	R20	T6		
					D4		
	L	L	L	L	L		

*Letters correspond to distances to be run or tasks to be performed listed on the corresponding Workout Sheet. Numbers denote the number of times the task is to be performed.

April					
A C	A F	A C	A F	A C	
X	V20	O20	V20	T6	
N6 L	L	Z6U L	L	N6 L	
May AC	AF	AC	AF	AC	
X	D6		D6	T6	
R8 V20	V10	R8 V20	V10		
S8 L	L	Q8 L	L		

Competitive Season—June through August

June			A F		
AC	AF	AC	F	AC	
X	P6	D6	R6	T6	
O10 V10	S8 Q10	U10 V10	S8 Q15		
	N6	Q2	N6		
L	L	L	L		
July† AC	F	AC	F	AC	
X	D6	D6	D6	D6	H
August‡ AF	AF	AF	AF	AF	
X	D6	D6	D6	D6	H

JAVELIN THROWER'S WORKOUT SHEET*

A   Warm-up: Jog ½ mile, exercises, 6 wind sprints
B   *Fartlek:* 2–3 miles
C   Weight room
D   Wind sprints on grass: Carry the javelin as in the approach
E   220 at ¾ effort: Concentrate on relaxation
F   Isometric exercises
G   660: Run distance between 2:25 and 2:40 (15-min. rest in-between)

†The program fluctuates from week to week during July and August. Schedules should be prepared on a weekly basis, depending on individual needs indicated during competition.

‡Emphasize speed and perfection of technique while maintaining the high level of physical conditioning thus far obtained.

*For an understanding of applying this sheet to a daily schedule, please refer to the table on page 265.

H	Competition
I	440: Easy
J	330: 7/8 to 9/10 effort (6-min. rest in-between)
K	220: 9/10 effort (5–7-min. rest in-between)
L	Warm-down: Jog 2 laps
M	80: From starting blocks
N	Starts: Out to 35 yards
O	Work on cross step using entire field: Cross, uncross, cross, uncross, etc.
P	Jab javelin in ground
Q	Throw from a stand with heavier javelin (men's)
R	Work on approach: Go into cross step (with javelin), a light easy throw
S	Total movement from approach to the release: Minimize the reverse
T	Throw: Measure and record
U	Emphasize lift and extension: Avoid fouling or falling off to one side
V	Concentrate on hip action throwing stance, smooth transfer from cross step to throwing; avoid fouling
W	Rest
X	Relay work
Y	50 yards (hard): Use standing start
Z	Straightaway intervals: Run straightaways, walk curves

JAVELIN THROWER'S SCHEDULE*

	Mon.	Tue.	Wed.	Thur.	Fri.	Sat.	Sun.
Preparatory Season—October through February							
October–November		A		A			
	C	F	C	F	C		
	B	D8	B	D8	B		
		L		L			
December–January		A		A			
	C	F	C	F	C		
	B	Z6	B	Z6	B		
	P16	O12	P16	O12	P16		

*Letters correspond to distances to be run or tasks to be performed listed on the corresponding Workout Sheet. Numbers denote the number of times the task is to be performed.

	L		L	
February	A	A	A	A	A
	C	F	C	F	C
	G1	P15	J2	P15	K3
		R10		R10	
	O10	S2	O10	S2	U10
					V10
	P12	D4	P12		
	L	L	L	L	L

Precompetitive Season—March through May

March	A	A	A	A	A
	C	F	C	F	C
	J2	S10	K2	S20–I2	
	Y6	R20	N6	R20	T6
					D4
	L	L	L	L	L
April	A	A	A	A	A
	C	F	C	F	C
	X	V20	Q20	V20	T6
	N6		U		N6
	L	L	Z6L	L	L
May	AC	AF	AC	AF	AC
	X				T

Competitive Season—June through August

June	AC	AF	AC	AF	AC
	X	P6	D6	R6	T
		S8	U10	S8	
	O10	Q10	V10	Q15	
	V10				
		N6	Q2	N6	
	L	L	L	L	

July†	AC	F	AC	F	AC	
	X	D6	D6	D6	D6	H

August‡	AF	AF	AF	AF	AF	
	D6	D6	D6	D6	D6	H

†The program fluctuates from week to week during July and August. Schedules should be prepared on a weekly basis, depending on individual needs indicated during competition.

‡Emphasize speed and perfection of technique while maintaining the high level of physical conditioning thus far obtained.

Index

Achievement, evaluation of, 139–140
Amateur Athletic Union (AAU), 2
American hop, in javelin throw, 111
Announcer, 192, 196
Approach:
  for high jump, 81–82, 89
  for javelin throw, 113–114, 117–118
  for long jump, 67–68
Arm action, in sprinting, 21–22, 24–25
Attire, 183–184
Audiovisual aids, 219–221
Awareness, in training, 170

Backward flop style, of high jump, 80, 87, 88
Ball throws, measuring distances, 210
Baton passing, 39–52
  common errors and corrections, 47–52
  in exchange zone, 43–44
  nonvisual, 40–42
  sample lesson plan, 162–167
  sprint pass, 44–45, 46
  teaching progression, 52
  visual, 45–47, 48–49
Block spacing, for starting, 8
Body lean and posture, in sprinting, 22, 25
Brumel, Valery, 88

Calisthenics, 176, 233–241
Checkmarks, for javelin throw, 113–114, 115

Chi Cheng, 17, 28
Chief finish judge, 203–204
Chief timekeeper, 204–205
Clerk of course, 192, 196, 200
Coaching, 169–179 (see also Training; Weight training)
  strategy for competition, 176–179
Competitive season, and training, 171–172
Conditioning, 28, 50, 135–136, 143, 177 (see also Training)
Conventional nonvisual pass, of baton, 40–42
Cross-country running, 32–38
  common errors and corrections, 37
  downhill, 33
  mechanical principles of, 36–37
  rules, 38
  strategy, 38
  teaching progression, 38
  techniques, exercises for, 33
  training schedule, 250–252
  uphill, 33–36
Cross-step, in javelin throw, 115–116, 118
Crouch start, 7, 8
Custodian, 193

Development, all-around, 169
Discus, 101–110
  common errors and corrections, 108–110
  drills, 146–147
  grip, 101, 102
  measuring distances, 209–211
  mechanical principles of, 106–108

Discus *(cont.)*
   rules, 110
   standing throw, 101–104
   teaching progression, 110
   training schedule, 262–264
   turn, 104–106
Distance running *(see*
     Cross-country running)
Division of Girls' and Women's
     Sports (DGWS), 2, 53

Eastern style, of high jump, 80
Eating habits, during
     competition, 178
Equipment, 132–134, 185–186
   improvising, 186–187
   for meet, 191
   suppliers, 218–219
Evaluation, of achievement,
     139–140, 161
Exchange zone, for baton
     passing, 43–44
Exercises:
   calisthenics, 176, 233–241
   isometric, 176, 231–233
   weight training, 224–228

Facilities, 184–185
Fartlek, 172
Field:
   events, 65–119
     discus, 101–110
     high jump, 80–91
     javelin throw, 111–119
     long jump, 67–79
     shot put, 92–100
   track and
     meet *(see* Meet)
     objectives of, 130–131
     participation outside of
       class, 2
     reasons for participation, 1
     sample teaching unit,
       141–161
     teaching of, 123–140

Field judge, 211–214
Field referee, 208
Finish judge, 204
Finnish style, 111 *(see also*
     Javelin)
Flight in air, in long jump,
     70–74, 78–79
Float style, in long jump, 72
Footwear, 183–184
Foreleg reach, in sprinting, 19–20
Form, good, in sprinting, 18
Fosbury, Dick, 81

Games Committee, 188, 193, 196
"Go" command, 11
Gradualness, in training, 170
Grip:
   in discus, 101, 102
   in javelin, 111–112
   in shot put, 92, 93, 98
   for weight training, 174
Groundskeeper, 191, 194

Half-miler, training schedule,
     248–250
Hang style, in long jump, 72,
     73–74, 75
Head field judge, 208–211
Heats, forming, 201
Henry, Franklin M., 12
High jump, 80–91
   approach, 81–82, 89
   bar clearance, 89–90
   common errors and
     corrections, 89–90
   drills, 146, 157–159
   measuring distances, 211
   mechanical principles of,
     86–88
   rules, 90–91
   straddle style, 80, 84–86, 88
   takeoff, 82–83, 89
   teaching progression, 90
   training schedule, 257–259
   Western roll, 83–84, 85

High knee action, in sprinting, 19
Hitch-kick style, in long jump,
    70–71, 72
Hurdling, 54–63
    common errors and
        corrections, 61–62
    drills, 145, 152–155
    mechanical principles of,
        60–61
    rules, 63
    strategy, 63
    teaching progression, 62–63
    training schedule, 253–255

Individualization, of training, 170
Inspectors, 192, 193, 195, 207
Interval training, 172–173
Isometric exercises, 176, 231–233

Javelin, 111–119
    approach, 113–114, 117–118
    checkmarks, 113–114, 115
    common errors and
        corrections, 117–119
    cross-step, 115–116, 118
    drills, 147–148
    Finnish style, 111
    follow-through, 116, 119
    grips, 111–112
    measuring distances, 209–210
    mechanical principles of,
        116–117
    rules, 119
    standing throw, 112–113
    teaching progression, 119
    training schedule, 264–267
Jones, Tom, 184
Judges, 192, 196, 203–204,
    208–214
Judges' stand, for meet, 191
Jump (*see* High jump; Long
    jump)

Kilborn, Pam, 54, 61

Landing, in long jump, 74–76
Larrieu, Frances, 34–35
Layout, in high jump, 83–86, 89
Leg action, in sprinting, 19–20
Long jump, 67–79
    approach, 67–68
    common errors and
        corrections, 77–79
    drills, 145–146, 155–157
    flight in air, 70–74, 78–79
    landing, 74–76
    measuring distances, 209, 211
    mechanical principles of,
        76–77
    rules, 79
    strategy, 79
    takeoff, 68–70, 77–78
    teaching progression, 79
    training schedule, 255–257

Marshals, 192, 196
Medley relay, 39
Meet:
    announcer, 196
    director, 188–189
    equipment and supplies, 191
    events and time schedule,
        189–191
    head groundsman, 190, 194
    officials, 192–193, 195–196,
        198–214
    organizing, 188–197
    program editor, 194
    public relations, 194–195
    safety precautions, 192
    seeding, 193
    ticket manager, 194
Meet card, samples, 212–213
Metric distances, equivalents of,
    221–222
Middle-distance running, 28–31
    common errors and
        corrections, 29
    drills, 145
    mechanical principles of, 29
    rules, 30

Middle-distance running *(cont.)*
strategy, 30–31
teaching progression, 29–30
Movements, in weight training, 175

Objectives, of track and field program, 130–131
O'Brien method, in shot put, 94–97
Officials:
for meet, 192–193, 195–196, 198–214
qualities of, 198
Officiating techniques, 198–214
Overload theory, 173

Pace, 30, 38
Plihal, Sally, 87
Point scores, 222–224
Precompetitive period, in training, 171
Preparatory period, in training, 171
Press steward, 193
Program editor, 194
Public relations, for meet, 194–195

Quarter-miler, training schedule, 246–248

Rallins, Mamie, 5–6, 58–59
Recorder, 192
Referee, 192, 195, 200, 208
Relaxation, in sprinting, 22–23, 25
Relay racing, 39–53 *(see also* Baton passing)
drills, 144–145
rules, 52–53
sample lesson plan, 162–167
strategy, 53

teaching progression, 52
Release, in shot put, 96, 99
Repetition, in training, 170
Reverse, in shot put, 96–97, 99–100
Running *(see* Cross-country running; Hurdling; Middle-distance running; Relay racing; Sprinting)
Running high jump *(see* High jump)
Russian style, in javelin throw, 111

Safety precautions, 134–135, 192
Scissors style, of high jump, 80
Score card, sample, 206
Scorer, 192, 196
Seeding, 193
Self-confidence, 178
"Set" command, 11
Shift, in shot put, 96, 99
Shot put, 92–100
action of, 94–97
common errors and corrections, 98–100
drills, 147, 159–161
grip, 92, 93, 98
measuring distances, 209–210
mechanical principles of, 97–98
O'Brien method, 94–97
rules, 100
sequences, 94–95
standing, 92–94
teaching progression, 100
training schedule, 260–262
Sprinting, 17–27 *(see also* Hurdling; Relay racing)
common errors and corrections, 24–25
drills, 144
good form, 18
mechanical principles of, 23–24
rules, 26

Sprinting *(cont.)*
strategy, 26–27
teaching progression, 26
training schedule, 243–246
Sprint pass, of baton, 44–45, 46
Stance in rear, in shot put, 96
Stances, for weight training, 174
Standing put, 92–94
Standing throw, of javelin,
112–113
Start, types of, 8 *(see also*
Starting)
Starter, 192, 195, 202–203
Starting, 7–16
commands, 8–12
common errors and
corrections, 13–15
drills, 150–152
mechanical principles of,
12–13
rules, 15–16
teaching progression, 15
technique, exercises for
learning, 11–12
Straddle style, of high jump, 80,
84–86, 88
Strength, development of, 173
Supplies, 134, 187
for meet, 191
sources, 218–219
Surveyor, 192

Takeoff:
for high jump, 82–83, 89
for long jump, 68–70, 77–78
"Take your mark" command,
9–11
Teaching of track and field,
123–140
appraising needs, interests,
and abilities, 131
culminating activities, 139
evaluating, 127–128, 139–140
events and skills, 138
facilities, equipment, supplies,
132–134

increasing interest, 132
lead-up, 135–136
lesson plans, 128–129
methods, 123–126
modified activities, 136–138
objectives, 130–131
planning units and lessons,
126–139
resource unit, 126, 129–130
rules, 139
safety precautions, 134–135
sample lesson plan, 162–167
sample teaching unit, 141–161
teaching unit, 126–129
Ticket manager, 194
Timekeepers, 192, 195, 204–205
Timing techniques, 205–206
Toussaint, Sandra, 28
Track:
events, 5–63
cross-country running, 32–38
hurdling, 54–63
middle-distance running,
28–31
relay racing, 39–53
sprinting, 17–27
starting, 7–16
and field
meet *(see* Meet)
objectives of, 130–131
participation outside of
class, 2
reasons for participation, 1
sample teaching unit,
141–161
teaching of, 123–140
Track and Field Guide, 184, 185,
194, 198, 199
*Track and Field Handbook and
Rules,* 185, 194, 199
Track referee, 200
Training, 169–176 *(see also*
Weight training)
developmental factors in,
172–176
general principles, 169–172
individualization of, 170

Training *(cont.)*
   periods, 171–172
   schedules, 242–267

Visual pass, of baton, 45–47,
   48–49

Weight training, 173–176
   essential information, 174–175
   exercises, 224–228
   period, length of, 175
   routine, 175
   schedule, 229–230
Western roll, in high jump, 80,
   83–84, 85
White, Wyllie B., 72–73